ID
THE DAYS OF MY YEARS

THE DAYS OF MY YEARS

an autobiography

by

DR. SAMUEL ROSENBLATT

Rabbi Emeritus of the Beth Tfiloh Congregation of Baltimore

Professor of Oriental Languages at the Johns Hopkins University

KTAV PUBLISHING HOUSE, INC.
NEW YORK
1976

© COPYRIGHT 1976
SAMUEL ROSENBLATT

Library of Congress Cataloging in Publication Data

Rosenblatt, Samuel, 1902-
  The days of my years.

    1. Rosenblatt, Samuel, 1902-   2. Rabbis—United States—Biography. I. Title.
BM755.R565A33   296.6′1 [B]   76-47616
ISBN 0-87068-494-9

A 937049

MANUFACTURED IN THE UNITED STATES OF AMERICA

Acknowledgments

As I offer these personal memoirs to the public, I feel that I must express my deep appreciation to the editors of the Jewish Times of Baltimore for allowing most of the material to appear in serial form in this widely read Anglo-Jewish weekly of the city which has been my home for almost half a century. I am beholden to two of the secretaries of the Beth Tfiloh Congregation, Mmes. Frances Levine and Lorraine Schlossberg, for typing the original text, in preparation for its publication week after week for an entire year. My sincere thanks go to the Ktav Publishing House, and especially its head, Mr. Bernard Scharfstein, for its splendid cooperation in the production of this volume and in taking care of all the technical details of format and appearance. I also appreciate deeply the encouragement given to this venture by many of the readers of "The Days of My Years" in the pages of the Jewish Times and the leaders of my beloved congregation and its brotherhood and sisterhood for their help in the distribution. However nothing can equal the value of the painstaking critique, advice and guidance of my dear life-partner Claire, who shared so many of the experiences related in this book.

Other books by the author

The High Ways to Perfection of Abraham Maimonides (N.Y. 1927)
The Interpretation of the Bible in the Mishnah (Balto. 1935)
The High Ways to Perfection of Abraham Maimonides II (Balto. 1938)
Our Heritage (New York 1940)
This is the Land (New York 1940)
The People of the Book (New York 1943)
The Book of Beliefs and Opinions of Saadia Gaon (New Haven 1948)
The History of the Mizrachi Movement (New York 1951)
Yossele Rosenblatt (New York 1954)
Hear, Oh Israel (New York 1958)
The Interpretation of the Bible in the Tosefta (Philadelphia 1974)
Under the Nuptial Canopy (New York 1975)

Contents

I.	Apologia	1
II.	Early Childhood in Pressburg	4
III.	We Move to Hamburg	7
IV.	Life in Hamburg	8
V.	The Ideal School	12
VI.	Leaving Germany	15
VII.	America: First Impressions	19
VIII.	Secular and Religious Education	22
IX.	I Become Bar Mitzvah	25
X.	High School Years	28
XI.	The Effects of the War	31
XII.	College Years	34
XIII.	The Jewish Theological Seminary	39
XIV.	Four Fruitful Years	42
XV.	Touring Europe	45
XVI.	Germany and Poland	48
XVII.	Slovakia and Westward	52
XVIII.	Columbia University	56
XIX.	Rabbi, Preacher, and Teacher	59
XX.	Courting Claire	62
XXI.	Hazard Fellow	65
XXII.	A Year in Jerusalem	69
XXIII.	Thinking of Claire and Home	75
XXIV.	My First Position	77
XXV.	Marriage	79
XXVI.	The Year in Trenton	82

XXVII.	Doctor of Philosophy	85
XXVIII.	Rabbi of Beth Tfiloh	87
XXIX.	Teaching Schedule	91
XXX.	Period of Apprenticeship	94
XXXI.	Laying the Groundwork	97
XXXII.	Molding a Congregation	101
XXXIII.	A Fateful Year	103
XXXIV.	Time Marches On	107
XXXV.	Father's Death	111
XXXVI.	To Visit Father's Grave	114
XXXVII.	Israel in 1934	117
XXXVIII.	Italy	121
XXXIX.	The 19th Zionist Congress	124
XL.	Recovery and Growth	127
XLI.	1935-1937	131
XLII.	Second Israel Pilgrimage	134
XLIII.	Impending Disaster	138
XLIV.	Life as Usual	141
XLV.	A Day School at Last	144
XLVI.	America Joins the War	147
XLVII.	Our Judah's Bar Mitzvah	149
XLVIII.	Saadiah's *Book of Beliefs*	151
XLIX.	Rabbinical Problems	154
L.	A Year of Decisions	156
LI.	Mission to South America	159
LII.	1948-1951	162
LIII.	Israel in 1951	165
LIV.	A Week in Morocco	168
LV.	Beth Tfiloh Celebrates My Silver Jubilee	171
LVI.	For the Sake of Israel	174
LVII.	Yossele Rosenblatt	176

LVIII.	For Bar-Ilan University	178
LIX.	Family Joys and Cares	181
LX.	At the Peak	184
LXI.	Portugal and Spain	188
LXII.	Change of Personnel	190
LXIII.	Last Year in Forest Park	192
LXIV.	Year of the Six-Day War	195
LXV.	Forty Years of Service	197
LXVI.	At Three Score and Ten	202
LXVII.	Epilogue	204

I

Apologia

BY THE TIME these pages appear in print I will have passed my seventy-fourth birthday. Nearly fifty-one years will have rolled by since the Jewish Theological Seminary of America bestowed upon me the title of Rabbi, Preacher, and Teacher in Israel. Almost half a century will have elapsed since I received from a rabbinical group in Israel, headed by the late Chief Rabbi Abraham Isaac Kook, the traditional ordination, or Semichah. Of the forty-nine and a half years that I have spent in the active rabbinate, I have served during all but one as the spiritual leader of the Beth Tfiloh Congregation of Baltimore. Upon my completion of the proverbial three-score years and ten, it elected me its rabbi emeritus for life.

Whatever the merits or lack of merits of my ministry may be, the very fact that I endured so long in one position, in an era of violent upheavals and a rapidly changing society, without compromising to any appreciable degree with the principles with which I set out on my career, is an indication that I must have done at least certain things right. If this is so, then the lessons taught me by experience might be of some value not only to my younger colleagues in the clergy but to laymen as well. To share these experiences, as I recall them, with those who might profit by them is the chief justification for committing to writing this account of "the days of my years."

First Question

Now the first question that the thoughtful reader of these memoirs might be moved to ask is probably: What was it that possessed me to enter a profession like the rabbinate? Was I not aware of the fact that as a public servant, expected to uphold the highest religious and ethical ideals, I would have but little privacy? Standing in the limelight, in which every flaw is accentuated and exaggerated, I would be an easy target for the carpers and critics on the sidelines, who like nothing better than to tear apart and snipe at those who are supposed to be their guides and mentors. Was this a job for a nice Jewish boy like myself? With all the opportunities offered by the world in which I grew up, for anyone with even a modicum of ability to attain material wealth and renown, could I not think of a better way of making a living than by becoming a rabbi?

The truth of the matter is that whoever enters the rabbinate, not as a means of earning a livelihood but as a life's vocation, a calling, does not do it so much from choice as out of inner compulsion. A person has to be born into it to make a success of it in the best sense of the word.

Scripture testifies concerning Jeremiah, who was typical of that most idealistic, selfless, and dedicated class of shepherds of men ever produced by the human race, the prophets of Israel, that he was destined for his role from birth. "The word of the Lord came unto me, saying: 'Before I formed thee in the belly, I knew thee, and before thou camest forth out of the womb, I sanctified thee. I appointed thee a prophet unto the nations.' " And once the divine call came to him, it burned within his breast like a consuming fire so that he was unable to restrain it.

The same applies to the spiritual heirs of the prophets, their present-day disciples who try to walk in their footsteps.

Rain or Shine

It seems that I was cut out for the rabbinate from my earliest youth by disposition, temperament, and inclination, as well as by environment, the home in which I grew up and the communities in which my parents lived. Even as a little boy I was more conscientious about the fulfillment of my religious duties, such as the recitation of the prayers upon awaking and before going to sleep, than any of my brothers and sisters. When I walked for the first time into the first-grade classroom of the Talmud Tora Realschule of Hamburg, Germany, where I received my elementary education, the old teacher, Herr Isaak, remarked to my father: "Your Samuel has such a serious look. Mark my words! He will one day be a rabbi." I had barely mastered the art of reading Hebrew when I became a regular attendant of the daily services in the chapel of our synagogue. Rain or shine, summer or winter, I would arrive there punctually at six o'clock in the morning, while my father, truly devout though he was—and he was known for his piety—was invariably late because he needed his night's sleep and rarely ever got to bed early.

The rabbis of the past were primarily scholars, men of learning. The very meaning of the title "rabbi" is not pastor or minister but teacher. As an apprentice for the rabbinate, I was anxious to follow the example of my illustrious predecessors in bygone generations. It was, therefore, inevitable for me to combine the love of Torah with the fear of heaven. All my life I have been a student. The acquisition of knowledge, the mastery of languages, the study of literature, science, and philosophy were my avocation. From the beginning of my school career, at the age of seven, until the end of my formal education seventeen years later, my grades were uniformly excellent, *ausgezeichent* in Germany, and A's or near the hundreds in high school and college in America. And during all that time, except for Jewish holidays, I missed only one-half day of class instruction.

II

Early Childhood in Pressburg

I WAS BORN on May 5, 1902, "three days after Passover," as my mother used to date my birthday. My father was at that time cantor of the Cultusgemeinde, the Orthodox Jewish community of Pressburg, now known as Bratislava, the capital of Slovakia. Slovakia was then a part of the kingdom of Hungary, and the city of Pressburg—Pozsony in Hungarian—was the chief religious center of Hungarian Jewry. There Rabbi Moses Schreiber (Chatam Sopher) of Frankfort on the Main, the most outstanding rabbinical scholar and talmudist of his time, had established his rabbinical school, or yeshivah, the fame of which spread throughout the world.

The atmosphere that prevailed in this celebrated institution of Jewish learning was one of deep piety coupled with a tinge of modernity. The vernacular used was a sort of Germanized Yiddish or High German, pronounced with a marked Hungarian accent. Many of the students were clean-shaven but used for the removal of their beards not a razor, which would have been a violation of the biblical prohibition in its literal meaning, but a chemical depilatory. They were frequent visitors at the home of my parents, and a number of them even boarded there. Several of them sang in my father's choir and later developed into first-class precentors of the synagogue. I recall a photograph featuring my father surrounded by his choristers (*meshorerim*) that hung on the wall of his study.

My birth, when my father was all of twenty years old, removed from my mother, who was a strikingly beautiful woman, the taunt of jealous Aunt Gittel, one of my father's sisters, that she was incapable of having children because she had produced no offspring during the first year of her marriage. As it happened, my appearance was followed by that of four other sons and three daughters, all of whom grew up to maturity. There are six of us still living today.

My recollections of the first four years of my life, during which I and my family resided in Pressburg, are rather vague. Raising me must have presented quite a hardship to my mother, because when I was one year old, shortly after my brother Leo was born, I broke out in an eczema of the skin, which caused me so much pain that I was perpetually crying. Fortunately the ailment left me, as our family physician had predicted, when I reached my third birthday. The rash disappeared as though it had never been. My skin cleared and has remained that way ever since.

"Mamma, My Gold"

I loved my mother dearly. "Mamma my gold" were the words in which I always addressed her. But I was also very much attached to my father. During the five years since his arrival in Pressburg, my mother had borne him two sons and a daughter. Since the congregation lacked the means for paying him a salary commensurate with the needs of his growing family, he was compelled to look elsewhere for a more adequate livelihood.

Just then the Synagogenverband (Union of Synagogues) of Hamburg, Germany, advertised for applicants for the position of cantor, which had become vacant. My father responded to the call. While he was away I missed him so much that, taking my younger brother Leo with me, I left the home of our maternal grandparents in Brzesko, Poland, where we were staying, to go looking for our father.

As soon as our absence was discovered, a posse was sent out in search of us by our frantic mother. We were found wandering in the woods outside the town. After we had been brought back home, a bit bewildered but safe and sound, I am told that I sang a sentimental ditty of my own composition, voicing my feelings of lonesomeness for my "Tateshu" and asking how long he would have to remain in Hamburg.

My father had been very happy in Pressburg. Everything about its atmosphere appealed to him. His art as a chazan was deeply appreciated, and he had every opportunity to express his emotions in the prayers of the synagogue without any restrictions, besides making the acquaintance of secular music, especially tenor arias of the most popular operas. He would never have left were it not for the necessity to improve his financial situation. His new position in Hamburg fulfilled that need, at the beginning at least.

For my mother our move to Hamburg came as a welcome relief from the shackles of her husband's family. She was no longer burdened with the care of a dying father-in-law besides performing all the duties of housewife and the mother of three children. She had her privacy, and was not exposed anymore to the harassment and carping of envious sisters-in-law, who begrudged her the good fortune of being their talented and greatly beloved brother's wife. Besides, as a product of the government schools of her native Galicia, where she had acquired a knowledge of both the Polish and German languages and their literatures, and taken courses in nursing, she welcomed the cultural opportunities furnished by Germany's chief seaport, as well as the orderliness and refinement of German Jewry. She loved to display her familiarity with the works of such outstanding German poets as Goethe and Schiller, whom she was able to quote at length.

Fenced In

It was quite different with my father. Although there was assuredly something admirable about the meticulous adherence on the part of the Orthodox elements of German Jewry to all the niceties of Jewish religious traditions, which was, of course, very much to his liking, he felt, as an artist, restricted, regimented, fenced in by the multitude of rules and regulations. How can a chazan who takes his art seriously give vent to his emotions in a prayer like the blessing of the New Moon, when he is forbidden to lament or to repeat such words as *parnosoh* ("sustenance")? Or how is it possible for a man, endowed by the Creator with a sensitive instrument so much in need of constant coddling as a voice, to be present at every synagogue function regardless of time or place?

Exterior of Synagogue in Pressburg, 1906

Interior of Synagogue in Pressburg, 1906

Exterior of Synagogue at Bornplatz, in Hamburg, Germany, 1906-1938

Interior of Synagogue at Bornplatz, in Hamburg, Germany, 1906-1938

III

We Move to Hamburg

FURTHERMORE, AS A WARM, compassionate human being, my father's heart went out particularly to his suffering brethren from Eastern Europe, who were then still passing in large numbers through the port of Hamburg on their way to America. Reared and raised in the lands of their origin, he was simply unable to either understand or stomach the apparent coldness of his German coreligionists, the complete restraint they displayed even in the face of such misfortunes as death.

All this did not affect his children. It passed us by completely. We were quickly transformed into full-fledged Germans. Notwithstanding the discrimination against adherents of the Jewish faith, which was still in force after the supposed political emancipation during the liberal era preceding the advent of the iron chancellor, Bismarck, most German Jews were ardent German patriots, whose devotion to the fatherland was second to none. In the private kindergarten run by Fräulein Lanzkron, to which we were sent prior to the beginning of our formal education in the boys' or girls' schools maintained by the Jewish community, we were taught not only the German national anthem but a whole assortment of songs extolling the heroism of the man of war. We were also drilled to march in line and keep in step like soldiers with sticks in our right arms in place of muskets.

We loved everything about our new surroundings, and there was, indeed, much in it that was bound to attract and impress us.

IV

Life in Hamburg

HAMBURG, AS WE KNEW IT between the years 1906 and 1912, was a beautiful, interesting, and, like most German urban centers at the time, clean city, in spite of the soot from the chimney stacks of the homes and the big coal-burning ocean liners in the harbor. The newer section, in which we resided, was crisscrossed by wide, tree-lined avenues flanked by imposing villas and spacious apartment houses. The older portion near the wharves, in which were located the first house of worship of my father's congregation, as well as its school, the temple of the Reformists, and the house of worship of the Spanish-Portuguese community, was quaint and most impressive, with wooden houses dating from the sixteenth century still standing on such streets as Kohlhöfen ("Coalyards").

The apartments we lived in, especially the last one on the Grindelhof, a short distance from the synagogue, were commodious, bright, and cheerful. They were warmed in the winter by tile stoves. Central heating had not yet come into vogue. The summers were usually mild, so there was really no need for air-conditioning.

We children loved to stroll with our father through such thoroughfares as Rotherbaumchaussee and along the Alster River front and under the nearby arcade known as the Esplanades. It was fun to ride in the ferryboat to the Uhlenhorst ferry house or to join the members of the choir on their annual excursions to Cuxhaven or Blankenese. It was exciting also to visit, in the old town of Altona north of the Elbe, the little cubbyhold of an apartment that she called home, of Fräulein Gumpel, the fifty-year-old practical nurse who took over whenever our mother was about to give birth to one of the four children that were added to our family during the six years of our stay in Hamburg.

Jewish Festivals

However, what intrigued us most of all was the manner in which the Jewish festivals of the year were celebrated. True, Hamburg was the cradle of German Reform Judaism. It was there that the first house of worship was erected by the Reformists. With these Reform Jews, however, we youngsters had no contact. All our acquaintances and friends were drawn from the ranks of the Orthodox. It was the garb that Judaism wore as *they* observed it that left its mark upon our young minds. It was indeed, to use a rabbinic expression, "the beauty of Japheth dwelling in the tents of Shem."

The daily morning and afternoon services were rarely ever attended by fewer than fifty worshippers. On Sabbath mornings the auditorium of the main sanctuary, a magnificent edifice, in the Romanesque-Moorish style of architecture, was filled almost to capacity. The men, clad in cutaways and striped trousers and full-length prayer-shawls, would have as their headgear silk hats. These they would pick up in the vestry in exchange for the homburgs or fedoras they would deposit there. On the High Holidays all the males in the synagogue wore white robes (kittels) and caps.

During the short interval between the Day of Atonement and the Feast of Booths, sukkahs, the wooden, foliage-covered huts called for as the temporary dwellings for the week of Sukkot, would suddenly spring up on the lawns or balconies of Jewish homes, most of them provided with roofs that could be lowered in the event of rain. The strains of hymns and psalms issuing from them during the holidays could be heard for blocks away. On Simchath Torah, the concluding day of the fall festive season, which is dedicated to the rejoicing over the Torah, the reading of which is then completed, the opening of the procession of the scrolls carried seven times around the synagogue presented an unusual spectacle.

Sweets for Weeks

My father, as the cantor and leader of these processions, would stand on top of the flight of twenty steps leading up to the Holy Ark facing the congregation as he held in his arm one of these scrolls. On both sides of him stood the lay leaders, each on a different step of the staircase, bearing a Torah. Then my father would intone the Sh'ma ("Hear, O Israel") to be followed by Ana Hashem Hoshiana ("O Lord, help, we pray"), and the march would begin. For the children, however, Simchath Torah was an occasion for the collection of candies and bonbons, which would be distributed liberally by the adult worshippers. I recall bringing back home one time enough sweets to last me and my brothers and sisters for weeks.

Chanukah meant, in addition to the kindling, in ascending order for eight nights in succession, of the Chanukah lamps, a menu of potato pancakes and the playing of games of chance with the use of the dreidel (spinning top). On Purim, besides listening to the reading of the Book of Esther (Megillah) on the evening and morning of the festival, we youngsters would become carriers of Shalach Manot, making certain that the mitzvah (injunction) of exchanging gifts of cakes and wines and other such edibles would be complied with. During the weeks before Passover every Jewish home would undergo a thorough house-cleaning. However, busiest of all was the Jewish community grocer, Herr Jakobsohn. Several days prior to the holiday, on which not only the eating, but the use of aught that is leavened, or contains the least admixture of chametz, is forbidden, he would close up his shop and open up, in several rooms of his residence, a complete stock of articles scrupulously kosher for Pessach.

Lag b'Omer, celebrating the end of the epidemic that had claimed the lives of many of the numerous disciples of Rabbi Akiba, who are believed to have served as soldiers in the army of Bar-Kochba, was a field day for the boys. Armed with bows and arrows, they would go out into the fields to test their skill in archery. On Shabuot, the Feast of Weeks, which commemorates the giving of the Torah at Sinai, the synagogue was decorated with palms, while at home dairy dishes, and especially cheesecake, would figure in the menu. No meat was eaten during the nine days ending with the Ninth of Ab. On that annual Black Fast, in mourning over the destruction of both the First and Second Temples of Jerusalem, the entire congregation would spend the morning in the synagogue, and all the men would be provided with low stools to sit on like mourners during the week following the death of a nearest of kin.

Thus all year round we had something to look forward to and keep occupied with; and busy children are happy children. As for myself, I became so much engrossed, when I was not yet six years old, under the inspiration of an artist friend of ours by the name of Geza Fisher, whom we knew from Pressburg, in the drawing of pictures of horses and houses, that I developed a writer's cramp. This necessitated the postponement of my formal education for an entire year.

However, I completely overcame my handicap, and, as noted previously, from the time I entered school until I completed the residence requirements for my doctorate at Columbia University and obtained my traditional ordination in the Land of Israel, my record of classroom attendance was near perfect.

V

The Ideal School

THE TALMUD TORA REALSCHULE, in which my father enrolled me shortly after I had reached my seventh birthday, was a model institution. It came as close as possible to the ideal of a Hebrew day school. It offered a complete program of secular as well as Jewish religious studies. I began to learn French and was initiated into the mysteries of algebra in my fourth school-year.

It was in April of 1912 that the school moved, from what had been its location for a century, in the courtyard of the old Kohlhöfen synagogue, to its new headquarters in the spacious, rectangular, solid, red-brick building erected by the community alongside the six-year-old sanctuary on the Bornplatz. It boasted, in addition to large, cheerful classrooms, furnished with the most up-to-date equipment, a gymnasium in which it was a joy to exercise. When the synagogue, like nearly all others in Germany, was razed to the ground by the Nazi storm-troopers during the fatal night of November 9, 1938, the school edifice was spared. Confiscated by the municipality, it is still standing today and, barring a bombing raid, may hold up for centuries.

As its designation, Talmud Tora Realschule, indicates, the courses in Jewish lore given at the institution were as important a part of the curriculum as the secular subjects. They included, besides Hebrew grammar, fluency in reading the prayers of the synagogue, the Bible and its commentaries, Jewish history and Mishnah, and the study in the upper grades of portions of the Talmud. As an aspirant rabbi, however, this did not quite satisfy me.

I did not have the patience to wait until I was about to graduate at the end of the nine-year course before taking a plunge into this sea of the wisdom of Israel's sages. So before I had reached my tenth birthday I enrolled in the Saturday-afternoon Talmud class conducted by Rabbi Seligmann Bär Bamberger of Würzburg, the rector of the klaus, or study-house, located at 11 Rutschbahn. I was the youngest of a group of about ten students anxious to quench their thirst for Jewish learning at this inexhaustible fount of knowledge.

Aside from being a man of erudition, Rabbi Bamberger was a warm, outgoing human being, who just beamed goodwill toward his pupils. Our text was the tractate of Betzah, which opens with a discussion of whether an egg laid on one of the major Jewish festivals is permitted to be eaten on that day. I can still see him with my mind's eye, after the lapse of nearly sixty-four years, this lovable, jovial, heavy-set, bekaftaned man in his early thirties with his round face adorned by a neatly trimmed red beard and mustache, expounding on the reasoning behind the varying views of teachers of the rival schools of Hillel and Shammai.

Drank Every Word

I also recall how eagerly I drank in every word that issued from his lips. He was like a perennially bubbling fountain, like a well that never ran dry. It would have been a great boon for me to have continued to study for at least several years under his tutelage and direction. But this was not to be, because, after I had attended his lectures only a few months, our sojourn of six years in Hamburg was terminated. For the second time within several weeks my father left for Bremen to board a ship bound for America, and this time it was for good.

He went in response to an invitation extended him by the First Congregation Ohab Zedek of New York to become its cantor. What lured him was the fact that the board of the Synagogenverband of Hamburg had turned down his request for an increase in salary, which he felt he needed to maintain his family. My mother had just given birth to her seventh child, my sister Sylvia. Burdened as he was in addition by his support of his recently widowed sister Gittel and his aged mother, he just could not make out with the seven thousand marks a year that was his total remuneration for his services. In view of the circumstances the offer of twenty-four hundred dollars per annum made him by Ohab Zedek was too tempting to resist.

Set to Depart

So right after Passover, which fell early that year, he filled a few valises with clothing and music and took the train to Bremerhaven. He was waiting for his ship to depart when the news broke of the *Titanic* disaster. At 2 A.M. on April 15, 1912, this largest ocean liner afloat, with a complement of more than twenty-four hundred passengers and crew, had struck an iceberg and was sunk, carrying over fifteen hundred persons aboard to a watery grave.

As if this was not enough, my father learned that his mother had just died. It was, of course, out of the question for him to travel during the mandatory seven days of mourning. So back to Hamburg he came. However, toward the end of May he set out again, and there was no more dissuading him and keeping him from reaching his destination.

After he had officiated the second Sabbath in the new sanctuary of the Ohab Zedek Congregation on 116th Street, with outstanding success, my father cabled my mother to sell the furniture, pack our personal belongings, and book passage for the family on one of the steamers of the Hamburg-Amerika line bound for New York.

VI

Leaving Germany

IT WAS MOST DIFFICULT to part with what had been our home for six years and in which the three oldest of us children, who were of school age, had become so firmly rooted that, although we were not born in the country, we looked upon ourselves as natives.

Germany was at that time, that is to say, prior to World War One, truly a land, nay *the* land, of Kultur. Illiteracy was nonexistent. The schoolmaster was highly revered. Next to the military, that of the teacher was the most respected of all professions. German scientists were in the vanguard of world scientific research. What they may have lacked in resourceful creativity, they made up for by thoroughness. A degree from a German university was a most coveted prize, because it was proof of real competence.

The study of Semitics, in particular, had become so widespread and was so diligently pursued in the institutions of higher learning in Germany, and the number of critical editions of Semitic texts turned out by the printing presses was so large, that it was remarked that German had to be a Semitic language since without it the acquisition of a knowledge of the Semitic dialects was impossible.

The German Reich of Wilhelm II of the house of Hohenzollern was a prosperous country. Its ships sailed the seven seas giving stiff competition to the number-one naval power, Great Britain. The output of its factories was very much in demand on account of the high quality of German manufactures. The trademark Made in Germany was a guarantee of excellence. The Germans had also begun to build up an overseas colonial empire. In Hagenbeck's famous zoo, located in

Hamburg, there were on display not only exotic and rare animals from all parts of the world, but also villages of natives of the Samoan Islands in the Pacific and of the Cameroons of South Africa.

Rabbis Were Scholars

All this was reflected in Germany's well-to-do, philanthropic, and cultured Jewish community. Even the non-Orthodox among the German rabbis were scholars, men of learning, and most of the Orthodox spiritual leaders boasted a Ph.D., evidence of their having obtained a modern university education. A considerable number were outstanding preachers and thinkers.

One of these, Dr. Anton Nobel, served as assistant rabbi in my father's synagogue prior to his departure for Frankfort on the Main. I remember hearing him when I was but eight years old. Although I was too young to follow the drift of his thoughts, he made a deep impression upon me by his eloquence, which Dr. Samuel Spitzer, who succeeded Dr. Markus Hirsch as chief rabbi, with his marked Hungarian accent and his old-fashioned method of sermonizing, could never equal. Juedische Wissenschaft—that is to say, the scientific investigation of the Jewish past—flourished in the rabbinical seminaries of Germany. The most comprehensive and authentic history of the Jewish people had been written by Professor Heinrich Graetz of the Rabbinical School of Breslau, and his methods were followed by other scholars.

On the board of our congregation there figured such distinguished personalities as Albert Ballin, the founder and head of the Hamburg-Amerika Line and an intimate of Kaiser Wilhelm. Another was the banker Max Warburg, a brother of Felix Warburg, who became a son-in-law of Jacob Schiff, America's leading Jewish philanthropist and one of the founding fathers of the reorganized Jewish Theological Seminary of America.

The membership of the Synagogenverband included a large number of physicians, lawyers, and successful businessmen. The teachers of the school, whatever unflattering nicknames may have been given them by their pupils privately, were held in high repute. The designation "Lehrer" was almost like a title of nobility.

Notwithstanding their rigid adherence to Jewish traditional law, the Orthodox Jews of Germany were men of the world. They were well versed in modern literature and science. They frequented the theater and the opera. Theirs was a far cry from the Orthodoxy of Eastern

Europe, which was completely untouched by the outer veneer of modern Western civilization.

Low Scholastic Standards

This is what we had to leave behind when we boarded the *Amerika* on June 26 of the year 1912 on our way to New York. My teacher in Talmud, Rabbi Bamberger, had tried very seriously to keep me in Hamburg. He had offered to make himself personally responsible for my maintenance. For if I wished to prepare for the rabbinate, the opportunites for becoming a rabbi worthy of the noble calling were then much greater in Germany than they were in the still very young and undeveloped United States of America, the scholastic standards of which were at that time certainly very much below those that prevailed in Germany.

However, my parents would not hear of being separated from me, their firstborn, notwithstanding the inducements. And it was fortunate that they turned down the offer. For had they accepted it, the outbreak two years later of World War One would have found me stranded in Germany, and they would have been worried sick over my safety and well-being.

As I stated previously, it was with much reluctance that we bade farewell to Hamburg. As our steamer was pulling out of the busy harbor of this second-largest urban center of our beloved Germany, which in accordance with the implication of the national anthem of "Deutschland, Deutschland über alles, über alles in der Welt," we considered superior to all other countries of the world, we bade a tearful goodbye to the fatherland in a sentimental wanderers' song, "Nun adee du mein lieb Heimatland"—"Farewell now, my dear homeland."

It took the *Amerika* ten whole days to cross the Atlantic Ocean. We were accompanied by my mother's youngest brother, Samuel Kaufman. He was later to become the chief cantor of Cracow, Poland. At the time of our departure he was still a bachelor. It was a good thing that he had come along, for it would have been next to impossible for my mother to keep track, all by herself, of her brood of seven children, ranging from the age of ten down to that of three months, this in addition to handling all the luggage we took along with us.

Second Class

We traveled second class. We devoured larger quantities of icecream than ever before in our lives. We also had our fill of seasickness. Because most of the oranges available on board were dry, I developed such a distaste for this vitamin-packed fruit that for several years I could not get myself to put an orange into my mouth.

On the Fourth of July, in honor of Independence Day, special festivities were held on our floating palace, as a sort of initiation into the spirit of the country that was to be our future home. However it was the sight, two days later, of the Statue of Liberty in New York Harbor that gave us the real feeling of what America was like and what it stood for.

Samuel at age 11
Leo at age 10

Samuel Rosenblatt at 16

VII

America: First Impressions

IT WAS A TENDER SCENE of reunion that unfolded at the pier of the Hamburg-Amerika Line, where father awaited us, when our ship docked there on the morning of July 6. Our family was together again after six anxious weeks of separation. This in itself was cause enough for rejoicing. Even more reason for such a feeling was it to see father's happy, smiling face. He appeared much more than satisfied with the change he had made.

The transfer from Germany to America represented for him true progress professionally as well as artistically. His position as cantor of the Ohab Zedek Congregation meant for him freedom from the restrictions that had been imposed upon him in Hamburg. It afforded him an opportunity to make full use of his talents whenever he was not occupied by the performance of his functions as precentor of his synagogue on Sabbaths and holidays.

It was quite different for the rest of us. Our initial impression of what was to be our home for the rest of our lives was far from favorable. First of all, the day of our landing happened to be one of the hottest of the year. The heat was unbearable. We had never experienced anything like it where we came from. There was no escape in this era, prior to the installation of air-conditioning, from discomfort in the congestion of America's number-one metropolis, which already then had a population of three million and the largest concentration of Jews in the world.

Secondly, compared to Hamburg, despite its soot, the New York that greeted us seemed filthy, untidy, and unswept. We were not accustomed to the litter and garbage strewn all over the streets, particularly in the less affluent sections of the city.

The reception we got from our father's oldest sister, Aunt Chava, a prematurely aging woman in her late forties and the mother of nine children with a tenth on the way, was very warm and cordial. But how poverty-stricken her modest little flat on East 106th Street, in which we were treated to our first meal in America, appeared to us. There was hardly any furniture aside from several metal bedsteads and a few tables and chairs. Uncle Nachman, her husband, who was already then ailing, was a bit of a freethinker.

It was not, therefore, surprising that the older children, who were already working, all of whom loved their parents dearly—I have seldom witnessed such devotion—were not Sabbath observers. Our conversation was in Yiddish, upon which we Germans looked down with disdain as a sort of corrupted German, a gibberish or jargon, not a real language. Though she had been in the country twenty years, Aunt Chava, who could neither read nor write, had not learned to speak English, and she never did acquire fluency in it.

Rats in the Drawers

The greatest disappointment of all, however, was the apartment that had been rented for us on the fourth floor of the tenement house at 2 West 119th Street, three short blocks from the synagogue. The six rooms of which it consisted were small and stuffy, half of them without sunlight, which was shut out by the wall of the adjacent building faced by the windows. There was hardly any space for beds or other household equipment. A musty odor prevailed because the place had apparently not been aired for quite some time. To top it off we discovered, on the morning after we had moved in, when we opened one of the drawers of the closets, a rat, something we had never seen before.

What a comedown from the bright, spacious, airy, beautifully decorated quarters on street level that had been our last residence in Hamburg. Is it a wonder that my mother complained, upbraiding my father for uprooting us from an environment of refinement, culture, and orderly living in order to dwell among rabble, riff-raff, people without traditions or manners or education?

In many respects our mother was right. America, at that time, was still a diamond in the rough. The standard of living of the overwhelming majority, that is, of the rank and file, was considerably below that of the civilized countries of Western Europe. Institutions of higher learning,

Jewish as well as non-Jewish, were few. Whoever was anxious to acquire a medical or rabbinical degree that stood for something would go to study in some European university to complete his education. It took two global wars for America to reach the intellectual heights achieved by the advanced states of Europe and even exceed them in technological and scientific progress.

Stifling Heat

The summer passed. Even though there was many a night on which it was next to impossible to sleep on account of the stifling heat, which continued long after sunset, we were able, since we were young, to live through it all without apparent damage to our health. Mother did the cooking—and an excellent cook she was, having learned in Germany how to prepare such delicacies as rhubarb pudding, fruit soups, salmon salad, and mayonnaise, and the most varied assortments of cookies, cakes, and pastry. To help in the housework she engaged Polish maids, with whom she communicated in the vernacular of her native Galicia. By listening to their conversation I managed to pick up a few Polish words and sentences.

When fall arrived and the summer vacation was over, the four oldest of us children—by that time our sister Gertrude was almost six—enrolled in the public schools of the vicinity. Mine was P.S. 10. I entered the fourth grade.

My English was, at the beginning, a bit weak, and the teacher, who possessed a smattering of German, was compelled occasionally to help me out by translating. However, within three months I had learned to express myself in the language of the classroom quite fluently, and what is more, I had lost every trace of a foreign accent. In fact, when I graduated three years later, making five grades within that period of time, I was awarded, among other things, the medal in grammar. It is still in my possession today.

VIII

Secular and Religious Education

LOOKING BACK from the vantage point of time upon the three years that I spent in the elementary grades of the American public-school system, I feel that I owe it a deep debt of gratitude. It was through it that I was first brought in contact with fellow Americans of every color and creed. It is true that my strict adherence to the Jewish dietary laws made too close an association between myself and my classmates virtually impossible. Nevertheless we learned to respect each other's idiosyncrasies and differences, to accept one another at our individual worth without prejudice and bias and develop that tolerance for nonconformists which is the glory of America. For myself, I can say that never in my entire career, public or private, did I experience what might be termed anti-Semitism. I do not know what sort of remarks may have been made in my absence. To my face, however, the behavior toward me of my non-Jewish superiors or colleagues has always been one of respect and deference.

It was natural that my closest friends during my school days should have been Jewish, though not necessarily observant Jews. In fact the one person, with whom I struck up an attachment that has endured until today, came from a family so completely assimilated that they did not even observe the Day of Atonement. George Robinton, who was about a year and a half my senior, was as different from me as could possibly be, physically as well as religiously.

My Friend George

He was a tall, handsome, strapping, blue-eyed six-footer, while I was a short, nearsighted, ash-blonde, who never grew beyond five-foot four.

Walking side by side we looked like Mutt and Jeff. He had no restrictions in the matter of food and one day of the week was like any other, while I ate only what was absolutely kosher and, of course, kept the Sabbath and the Jewish holidays. Nevertheless, we got along together marvelously. We had a lot to talk about, discuss, and debate. What we shared in common was a thirst for knowledge and a deep interest in the study of history and geography.

Once, I was then about sixteen, George proposed that we spend a week on a farm owned by a Yankee farmer he knew, not far from Poughkeepsie. I took along a few pots and pans in which to prepare my food while he acted, as he did on occasion later on, as my Shabbos goy. We had ourselves a delightful vacation, and everybody seemed pleased with the experience. George and his fiancée, Beatrice Marblestone, were the first couple to be united by me in wedlock. I performed the marriage rites of their two children. I also participated several years ago in their golden wedding anniversary. Though he never changed his basic mode of living, he did affiliate with Temple Emanuel of New York, which was more than his father, a veteran of the Spanish-American War, whose brothers in Russia had all married out of the faith, ever did. His son, Andrew, celebrated his Bar-Mitzvah at the age of thirteen. George himself had never gone through this ritual of initiation into the responsibilities of Jewish adult life.

My three years at P.S. 10 laid the foundation of my secular education in America. Although the standards were not as high as were those that obtained at the Talmud Tora Realschule of Hamburg, the results were, on the whole, quite satisfactory. Except for the principal and the science instructor, Mr. Birch, who was a bit of an eccentric, all my teachers were women, and my rapport with them was excellent. My scholastic record for the six semesters was a straight A. My brothers and sisters, all of them received their elementary training at P.S. 84 on 116th Street, across the street from the synagogue, and some of them were excellent students.

Everything in Yiddish

The efforts of our parents to make provision for our Jewish religious education did not run quite so smoothly. The only educational institution in our neighborhood that offered a curriculum parallel to its equivalents in Hamburg was the Yeshivah of Harlem on 114th Street. However, the decorum and discipline in this elementary Hebrew day school was poor. The place was neither orderly nor clean. Worst of all, however, was the fact that the language of instruction for all the Hebrew and religious courses was Yiddish, which we detested. It was for the same reason that I and my brother Leo quickly tired of the classes in Bible, prayers, and Jewish history held in the late afternoons and early evenings, three hours in succession on five days every week, at the Salanter Talmud Torah on East 118th Street. The use of Yiddish in translating the Hebrew text offended our classic German ears and turned us off. As a last resort, father engaged a private Hebrew teacher, who had his one-room school on the second floor of an apartment house on Fifth Avenue near 115th Street. Mr. Weisbart was a Warsaw Hebraist, as well versed in German as he was in English. His forte was Hebrew grammar and Bible. He also possessed considerable expertise in the knowledge of the Talmud.

Hebrew Groundwork

It was I, more than the rest of my generation of Rosenblatts, who took advantage of what Mr. Weisbart had to offer. I accumulated, under his guidance, a considerable Hebrew vocabulary. I became acquainted with all the fine points and niceties of Hebrew grammar. I became fluent in the reading of the historical books of the Bible and in appreciating the eloquence of Isaiah and the rhetoric of Job. It was Mr. Weisbart who introduced me to the romantic works of such pioneers of modern Hebrew literature as Abraham Mapu and Perez Smolensky, whose novels so fascinated me that I was just unable to tear myself away once I had begun reading them. So deep an influence did they exert upon me that I soon began to imitate their style in a tale about the exploits of a Rabbi Jonah that I composed.

IX

I Become Bar Mitzvah

THANKS TO MR. WEISBART'S excellent coaching, my own eagerness to learn, and the fact that I had inherited from my father an ear for music, a resonant voice, a good sense of pitch, and a clear enunciation, I was well prepared for my performance in the synagogue on the Sabbath of my Bar Mitzvah.

The celebration of my initiation into adulthood as a Jew took place on the Saturday immediately following Passover, when the prayer for the New Moon that ushered in the month of Iyar was recited. On such occasions, when it was known that my father, who was then already at the height of his profession, would officiate, the main auditorium of Ohab Zedek, which had become the spiritual home of the aristocracy of New York's Orthodox Jewry, would be filled to its capacity of nearly two thousand worshippers. Some came from as far away as San Francisco to hear the "Jewish Caruso."

There were times when it was necessary to charge a price of admission just to prevent disorders due to overcrowding. This applied particularly to the annual Selichot, the predawn penitential service on the Sunday preceding the Jewish New Year. The entire block of 116th Street, between Fifth and Lenox Avenues, on which the synagogue was located, would be black, from 2 A.M. on, with people hoping to be able to get in. Seats for the High Holidays were sold out weeks in advance and additional chairs had to be set up in the aisles.

Is it a wonder that the schul should have been full to overflowing on the Sabbath on which Yossele Rosenblatt was celebrating the Bar Mitzvah of his firstborn, the oldest of his eight children? My father was in excellent form that day, in his very best mettle. His face was beaming as he listened to me chanting first the entire weekly portion of the Torah and then the Haftarah, or message from the Prophets, each in the special intonation prescribed by tradition. My happiness was complete when Dr. Philip Klein, the venerable rabbi of the congregation, stated in his remarks to me that he had never heard the words of Scripture read with such correctness and attention to every grammatical detail.

Before the Mussaph (additional) service I made my maiden appearance as a public speaker. I delivered no less than three short addresses, one each in Hebrew, English, and German. The last was entirely my own composition. I experienced no stage fright whatever, and my audience seemed to be impressed.

Treasured Gifts

Among those present at the time was my future father-in-law, Isser Woloch. He had just moved to Harlem from the Bronx, where he had resided for half a year since his arrival on the last ship to cross the Atlantic from Belgium at the outbreak of World War I. He had joined Ohab Zedek because he wanted his children to grow up in an atmosphere that would make them develop a love for Judaism.

On the Sunday following this gala Sabbath, we had open house in honor of the event in our third rented apartment since our arrival in the United States. It was located on the fourth floor of 100 West 114th Street, whither we had moved from 2 West 117th Street. It was more spacious, cheerful, and brighter than its predecessor and afforded a beautiful view of the neighborhood.

Among the gifts that I received upon "becoming a man" that I treasure to this day, in addition to the gold Waltham watch from my parents with a Hebrew inscription composed by my teacher, Mr. Weisbart, were the six volumes of Graetz's *History of the Jews* given to me by the vice-president, Mr. Borenstein. My library was enriched also by the complete works of the German-Jewish poet Heinrich Heine in the deluxe Elster edition, presented by an old friend from Hamburg and music lover. Mr. Nathan Gruenwald.

It was almost two years since my mother had borne her last and eighth child, my brother Ralph. He was the only native American among the offspring of Josef and Taube Rosenblatt. I was very much attached to the little fellow. As the oldest brother, I often wheeled him around in his carriage, thereby relieving my mother, who was busy taking care of the rest of the family. To this day I am in close contact with him. He keeps me posted on the doings of the remainder of my brothers and sisters, all of whom live in or around New York.

Father was, in those days, not yet as busy with engagements that compelled him to travel all over the United States as he became later on. He still had time to visit relatives and friends living on the East Side, the first center of Jewish population of the metropolis, as well as the Brownsville section of Brooklyn and the Bronx.

Occasionally I would accompany him, using either the subways or the el (elevated railroad). In this way I made the acquaintance of neighborhoods of the sprawling city other than the one in which we lived. They were not the most affluent and well kept, to be sure. Yet it was there that most of the millions of New Yorkers had their homes.

Among the celebrities whom he took me to see around that time of my life was Professor Solomon Schechter, the real architect of the Jewish Theological Seminary of America, which I was to enter six years later for my rabbinical training.

Our interview with him took place shortly before his passing. Though I do not recall the nature of my father's conversation with him, the mere encounter made the deepest impression on me. I can still visualize the leonine head, the piercing eyes, the full red beard, and the sparkling wit that made him so outstanding.

His contributions to Jewish learning, not the least of which was the unraveling of the treasures of the Cairo Genizah, which he had discovered, were enormous. But perhaps even greater was the service he rendered to American Jewry by bringing to the institution upon which he had put his imprint such scholars as Louis Ginzberg, Alexander Marx, and Israel Friedlander. The first two of them were to become my teachers.

X

High School Years

UPON MY COMPLETION of my elementary education, I entered Townsend Harris Hall, which was the preparatory department of the College of the City of New York, the new headquarters of which, on 138th Street and Amsterdam Avenue, had only recently been completed. It was a high school to which only superior students were admitted, for it compressed into three years a curriculum which normally required four years to cover. Ninety-five percent of the student body, like that of City College itself, which was a free school under municipal auspices, were at that time Jewish. It consisted of either immigrants or children of immigrants.

I excelled in all my studies, winning prizes for Latin and French and a medal for algebra and geometry, in which I scored a perfect mark. Townsend Harris was an all-male school. French was taught by native French instructors, so I was able to acquire a real Parisian accent in speaking the language. I received my grounding in Latin from Dr. Samuel Pearl, a young Jewish teacher for whom I had a deep affection, a feeling which was fully reciprocated.

Shortly before my graduation at the age of sixteen, the Balfour Declaration was issued. Ardent Zionist that I had been from my earliest youth, I delivered, before my classmates, an impassioned oration on the significance of this epoch-making pronouncement, which for the first time in history voiced the recognition by a world power of the Jewish people's claim to what had once been its national home. It earned me the award of my first prize for oratory.

An account of the honors bestowed upon me on my graduation from Townsend Harris at the age of sixteen appeared in several periodicals. One of them was *Musical America*. The weekly of American music lovers, it often carried items of personal interest about Josef Rosenblatt, the modest singer of the synagogue who had leaped into international fame by his rejection of the offer made by Cleofonte Campanini, director of the Chicago Opera Company of one thousand dollars a night for the role Elazar in *La Juive*.

The meeting between my father and the opera impresario took place after one of the concerts given by my father in the early spring of the year 1918 for the benefit of Jewish war sufferers. It was a year since, shortly after the reelection of President Woodrow Wilson, on the promise of keeping it out of the first global conflict, our nation decided to cast its lot with the Allies, who were then hard-pressed by the Germans. While our entry into the fray cost us many a precious American life and much substance, it brought victory to the arms of the victims of aggression.

We were hailed as the saviors of humanity, who had made the world free for democracy. Its participation in the war also made our United States the leading military and economic power on earth. The now four million Jews safely ensconced in the land of the free, became thereby the big brothers and chief prop to lean on of the sorely stricken Jewish communities of Europe.

Growing Affluence

As a consequence of the growing affluence of the American nation in general, which was one of the byproducts of the war, by which the Western Hemisphere had been completely untouched, the material fortunes of our family also improved. Differences now arose between my father and his congregation not so much over his salary as his freedom. By threatening to leave Ohab Zedek, he was able, after his five-year contract had run out, to extract from the congregation the right to accept engagements to officiate elsewhere on a minimum of two Sabbaths a month.

Then, after the recognition his talents had won for him from connoisseurs of the caliber of a Cleofonte Campanini, my father's stock went up to the point where his remuneration for concerts increased fivefold. Even before this had happened, we had moved from our flat at 100 West 114th Street to a four-story house at No. 50, the middle of a block that boasted no less than ten houses of worship, large and small, including the Yeshivah of Harlem.

We had enough room now for a maid and cook to sleep in. We were able to offer hospitality to an aspiring young chazan, fresh from the Russian Ukraine, who became one of my father's star pupils, Samuel Malavsky. It became possible for us to rent a cottage not far from the beach in the resort town of Long Branch, New Jersey, in which to spend the months of July and August bathing and breathing in the fresh sea air, and thus escaping the intense summer heat, coupled with congestion, of the city.

XI

The Effects of the War

THE BLOODY CONFLICT, which had exacted a proportionately heavier toll from the Jews of Eastern Europe than from any other group, came to an end on November 11, 1918, which has since been observed as Armistice Day. However, before the conflagration had burned itself out, it imported to our country, which had escaped the ravages of war, a malady more devastating than the war itself, the "flu".

Of our own family, all except father and sister Nettie were stricken. Our house resembled a hospital. Mother, because of her training as a nurse, went from bed to bed to attend the sick, until she herself succumbed and professional nurses had to be engaged to take care of us.

Worst off of all was our guest, Samuel Malavsky, who on top of the flu had contracted pneumonia. Fortunately, we all recovered, although we learned that the undertakers and grave-diggers had been working overtime to bury the unusually large number that had died from the much dreaded influenza.

School Closed

On account of the epidemic, the College of the City of New York, which I was scheduled to enter early in September, opened two weeks late. This kept me from missing classes and thus spoiling my record of attendance. During the first semester, instruction was given in the century-old building on 23rd Street and Lexington Avenue. For the second, the college returned to its newer headquarters on 138th Street and Amsterdam Avenue.

It was then that I first met Simon Greenberg, my classmate and closest friend during my four years as a rabbinical student at the Jewish Theological Seminary. What attracted me to him was his scintillating mind, his sincerity and dynamism, qualities that made him later on an effective preacher and outstanding leader, and, after a successful career in the active rabbinate, elevated him to the vice-chancellorship of his alma mater and the presidency of the University of Judaism on the West Coast.

Another member of my class in City College was Simon H. Rifkind, a distinguished jurist, who is presently chairman of the executive committee of the Jewish Theological Seminary. We studied American history together and competed for the same prize in that subject.

A Bit of Drilling

Although I was a humanities major, I was the only student taking Professor Baskerville's course in chemistry during the freshman year to receive a grade of over ninety percent out of a class of 250, half of whom flunked. Since the war did not end until November 11 of that year, I was virtually compelled, as were all of my classmates who were not conscientious objectors, to don the ROTC (Reserve Officers Training Corps) uniform. We did a good bit of drilling, marching, and shouldering of arms. However, we had not had a chance to get as far as target practice when the shooting was over and military training was no longer necessary. It was my good luck to have been too young to be drafted into the army during the First World War and too old to be called to serve when our country joined the second global conflict twenty-three years later.

The outbreak of hostilities in Europe in the fall of 1914 had brought to our shores a number of Jewish celebrities, with whom I had the good fortune of becoming personally acquainted. This was due to my father's deep interest in the causes they represented, and to his renown as a cantor who, by his vocal art, gave expression to the innermost feelings of his people, its joys as well as its sorrows.

An Author's Kiss

One of these was the Jewish Mark Twain, known by his pen-name of Sholom Aleichem. The most popular musical of our generation, *Fiddler on the Roof*, is based on his character Tevyeh, the Dairyman. Sholom Rabinowitz had no sooner arrived in New York from his native Russia than he made it his business to worship in our synagogue, the Ohab

Zedek. I recall distinctly how this prematurely aging man in his fifties, with his wrinkled brow, black gabardine, and tattered old silk hat, at the conclusion of the Friday evening service walked up to the bema (platform) in the front of the pulpit of the sanctuary. Before my father had a chance to come down, he planted a kiss on his forehead in recognition of a most masterful rendition of the ancient prayers.

Another one of European Jewry's great, who often visited us in our home, was Rabbi Meir Berlin, the leader of the Religious Zionists and founder of the American branch of the Mizrachi movement. He was a gifted writer and preacher, a man who always had something to say and did it most persuasively and convincingly. One of the architects of the State of Israel, he was still among the living when its birth was announced. He laid the foundation of the *Talmudic Encyclopedia* and was the inspiration for the Bar-Ilan University in Ramat Gan, which was named after him.

A close colleague and collaborator of Rabbi Berlin's, who took refuge in the United States during the war years, barely missing arrest by the Turkish authorities, was Rabbi Judah Leib Fishman. Under the name of Maimon he became Israel's first minister of religions in the cabinet of David Ben-Gurion. I met him at the Mizrachi headquarters on New York's East Side. A prolific author, writing Hebrew with a pithy style, his pronunciation of the sacred tongue was that of his native Bessarabia. When he addressed a Zionist gathering, at which I had the privilege to preside in Baltimore after the establishment of the Jewish state, he referred to himself as *sar hadooses* instead of *sar hadatot*. It brought a smile to our local Hebraists.

XII

College Years

THE PLIGHT of East European Jewry as a result of the First World War gave rise to the birth of two nationwide American Jewish organizations that are still in existence today. One was the Joint Distribution Committee, the function of which was philanthropic. The other was the American Jewish Congress, the aim of which was political, the securing of Jewish rights. The leading figure of the first was Jacob Schiff. It was he who had sparked the campaign for the largest sum ever raised out of private means for purposes of relief by contributing the unprecedented amount of half a million dollars.

I had the unique privilege of meeting him in person when my father gave a concert for the benefit of the patients at the Montefiore Hospital of New York, of which this patron of a whole legion of Jewish causes was one of the chief benefactors. The other was founded by Dr. Stephen S. Wise, the most powerful voice for nearly two generations of American Jewry. His eloquence and warm Jewish heart were greatly admired by my father. He in turn entertained the highest regard for his admirer. I had the pleasure of being host to him in my home on an evening when he graced the forum of my congregation in Baltimore.

Macy's and Milk

Another outstanding American Jewish philanthropist, with whom I was brought in contact by virtue of being a son of Yossele Rosenblatt, was the merchant prince Nathan Straus, owner of Macy's, the world's largest department store. It was he who saved the lives of thousands of American babies by opening free milk stations in the city of New York.

Together with my parents and my brother Leo, I was invited, on a bright and sunny day in June of the year 1919, to the elegant Straus mansion in Mamaroneck for luncheon. It was a most delicious fish meal, prepared specially for us Rosenblatts and served on brand new china. I still remember the cheerful, blue-tiled dining room into which we were ushered and the gracious hospitality of the patriarchal couple. I recall also the embarrassment of my brother Leo when the tight pants he wore split and there was neither time nor opportunity to change them.

Future Wife

As for extracurricular activities during my college years, I joined the Menorah Society, then the leading Jewish student organization at CCNY. I was also a member of the Cercle Jusserand, a French-speaking club. It was there that I was thrown together with the little girl who was to become my wife. The first time I met Claire was at the Bar Mitzvah of her brother Nathan, a year and a half her junior. It was her father, the little Frenchman of our synagogue, with whom I loved to practice my French, who had invited me to Kiddush after synagogue services on the day of his son's celebration of his coming of age as a Jew.

I wonder whether he then already had a premonition that I would one day become his son-in-law. Claire was a very attractive, slender brunette, with beautiful soft brown eyes, lovely black tresses, a caressing voice, and a warm personality. That she was intelligent, the possessor of a keen and analytical mind, coupled with good common sense and an interest in human beings, I had an opportunity to discover during our walks on Sabbath mornings, when we met on the way through Central Park to the Jewish Center to hear the sermons of Rabbi Leo Jung.

Right from the outset, shy as I was, I felt at home in Claire's company. It was as though an invisible, yet irresistible, bond drew me to her. Yet it was not until several years later, after I had received my rabbinical degree, that I first began to court her. In the interim, I was too busy preparing for my future to take time out for dating young women or participating seriously in social functions leading to marriage. All my leisure hours were devoted to preparing for my career by the acquisition of knowledge.

Bustling House

It is still a mystery to me today how I managed to concentrate in a place as busy and noisy as our new home was at 50 West 120th Street. The four-story brownstone row house, facing a corner of Mount Morris

Park, acquired by father in 1920 with the help of a substantial mortgage, and elegantly furnished by mother, was almost like 42nd Street and Broadway. People were coming in and going out in a seemingly endless stream.

The individuals who frequented the Rosenblatt household were of every type and description. There were among them schnorrers, who showed up with regularity at the beginning of every Jewish month for handouts. There were cantors like Kwartin, Roitman, Rutman, and Karniol, and later on Chagi and Alter, opera singers of the type of Joseph Schwartz of Vienna, and choir directors Wohl, Posner, and Machtenberg. Whenever they got together, there was singing and concertizing. Among our visitors, one who stayed at our home for several weeks during his sojourn in the United States was a Cantor Einfeld from Australia.

Among the guests whom we were privileged to entertain, were Jewish intellectuals of the caliber of Professor Israel Friedlander of the Jewish Theological Seminary of America. He was murdered by hooligans in the Ukraine in 1921 while on a mission of mercy on behalf of the American Jewish Joint. In addition, there were hosts of admirers and others who just attached themselves to us and forgot to leave. We never sat down to a meal without some strangers, whether invited or uninvited, joining us. My parents just did not have the heart to even hint to them to leave.

The only way it was possible for me to study was to isolate myself by going upstairs to the library, which served also as the bedroom of myself and my brother Leo. Once there, I shut myself out from the world surrounding me as though it did not exist. The house could have burned down, so my sisters and brothers tell me, without my being aware of what was happening.

An Avid Reader

I was an avid reader, never without a book. Besides studying the Talmud, I read Bible commentaries, history, philosophy and sociology. But my chief hobby was languages. The goal I had set for myself was to learn at least one foreign tongue during the interval between the end of every school year and the beginning of the next, while vacationing with the family in Long Branch. In this way I taught myself Italian and classical Greek. I also covered enough of Spanish literature to be able, after a year of elementary Spanish, to take Professor Arbib Costa's advanced course in Cervantes' *Don Quixote*.

When it was brought to my attention that I could shorten the time I would normally have had to spend in college by one semester by passing an examination in German, I dedicated the summer prior to my last year at City College to going through a German grammar and making a study of the works of Lessing, Schiller, and Goethe. I was tested by the head of the German department, Professor Von Klenze, awarded eighteen credits for the work done, and then had the pleasure of reading Goethe's *Faust* under his expert guidance. Von Klenze, who spoke a flawless English, was a pacifist during the war period. He was known as a liberal socialist and a friend of Jews. After the war, he returned to his native Germany. The next thing we heard about him was that he had joined the Nazi party and become one of its most virulent leaders.

"C" in Gym

It was the practice in those days in City College to award extra credits for A's and B's. This enabled me to reduce my residence requirements by another half-year and obtain my baccalaureate in a total of three instead of the usual four years. I came near spoiling my record on account of the subject called gym. Though I was blessed with a pretty sturdy constitution, athletics was never my forte. I had practiced wrestling for a while only to give it up before very long; and I quickly tired of bicycle riding. The highest mark I was able to obtain for physical prowess was a C. Fortunately the course was coupled with hygiene, which was purely mental. This raised my average to a B. But then another problem presented itself. In order to graduate, I had to swim the full length of the college swimming pool. I had never tried it before. But since I knew it had to be done, I jumped into the water. Though I nearly drowned in the act and was half-dead when I reached my destination, I made it.

At the age of nineteen I graduated, leading the Phi Beta Kappa list, at the head of a class of 333, and carrying off prizes for Latin, Spanish, and German. I was awarded second honors for oratory, first place having been taken by a Negro classmate, with whom I had shared a bench in the public-speaking class. Though my average should have entitled me to Summa Cum Laude, I rated only Magna Cum Laude on account of an insufficient number of actual residence credits.

Pondering a Career

It was a very proud day for my parents that day in June of the year 1921 on which I walked off with my sheepskin, inscribed with the first academic degree, from the stage of the Great Hall, which had twice been filled to overflowing when father had given a concert in it. And now that my college education was completed, the question I had to ask myself was, What next?

For a while I had been diverted from my original intention of entering the rabbinate by toying with the idea of studying international law. However, during the summer following graduation, I chanced to meet, at the beach of Long Branch, Professor Mordecai M. Kaplan. He had already then made a reputation for himself as one of the most original, albeit disturbing, thinkers in the American rabbinate, even though he had not yet fully formulated his Reconstructionist philosophy. I had attended, at his home, several sessions in higher Bible criticism, and it was he who persuaded me to enroll in the Jewish Theological Seminary and become a rabbi.

Father Disappointed

My father was somewhat disappointed at my choice. He would have preferred the Rabbi Isaac Elchanan Rabbinical Seminary, whose president was then Dr. Revel, whom he greatly admired as a scholar and a friend. But when I told him that the Jewish Theological Seminary was better qualified to provide me with the polish needed to succeed as the spiritual leader of an American congregation, and that I could remain true to Orthodoxy even as a graduate of that institution, especially since thirty percent of the communities then affiliated with the United Synagogue were Orthodox in practice, he gave in.

And so, in the fall of 1921, I became a student at the Jewish Theological Seminary of America. Founded in the year 1886 by the Italian-born Rabbi Sabato Morais, as an antidote against American Reform Judaism, it was reorganized in 1902 by Dr. Solomon Schechter, a native of Rumania, who had been trained in the rabbinical seminary of Vienna and served as reader in rabbinics at Cambridge University prior to coming to America.

XIII

The Jewish Theological Seminary

I WAS NOT DISAPPOINTED. The seminary fulfilled all my expectations. True, the courses offered by it, and the lectures given by the members of its distinguished faculty, did not put the stress laid by the Orthodox rabbinical schools on the fine points of Jewish law. Nor was there demanded of its fledglings the concentration, to the almost complete exclusion of other disciplines, on the exhaustive study of the Talmud and its commentaries. Yet was there opened to me the door to nearly all branches of Jewish lore.

Louis Ginzberg

Professor Louis Ginzberg was by far the keenest mind and the most brilliant scholar in the galaxy of outstanding thinkers and men of learning of which the teaching staff consisted. A descendant of that foremost talmudist of the eighteenth century, Rabbi Elijah of Vilna, known popularly as the Vilna Gaon, he followed, in his method of exploring the works of the tannaim, the amoraim, and their successors the ways of his illustrious ancestor. Among these was a critical examination of all available texts.

A native of Lithuania and a product of its yeshivot, he had acquired, during his childhood years and his early adolescence in these centers of traditional Jewish culture of Eastern Europe, a complete mastery of both the Babylonian and the Palestinian Talmud. To this he was able to add, as a result of his later training in the universities of Germany and Holland, what light could be thrown on these classics of Jewish belief and practice by the teachings of modern science, philosophy, and history, as well as comparative Semitic philology.

He already had to his credit, when I became his pupil, his monumental *Legends of the Jews*, the *Geonica* (history of the Geonim, the heads of the academies of Babylonia in the post-talmudic era), and countless contributions to the *Jewish Encyclopedia*. His elucidations of the texts of the tractates of the Talmud, on which he discoursed several times a week, were real eye-openers. They made the oft-clashing views of the ancient authorities quoted so vivid and logical that they seemed almost like contemporaries. They afforded the listener an opportunity to peep behind the utterances, see the contexts in which they were made, and recognize the situations that prompted them. The world of the Talmud became alive. It became possible to trace the developments in Jewish as well as general history that had led to the enactment of measures adopted. These included the means taken to improve the status of women, cope with changing economic conditions, enhance the enjoyment of the Sabbath and festivals, and combat a hostile environment.

Alexander Marx

German-born Alexander Marx, who taught Jewish history, was an excellent complement to Professor Ginzberg. A specialist in book-lore, whose eyes were open to whatever had been published that was of Jewish interest, he was not only the architect and builder of the seminary library, the largest and most complete of its type in its day in the world, and the Mecca of Jewish scholars. He was himself a walking encyclopedia, whom whoever wished to do research in any field of Jewish knowledge had to consult for the sources. He was distinguished not only for his learning, kindness, and modesty, but also his piety. I had occasion to see him on Sabbaths and holidays at the Ohab Zedek Synagogue, where he often came to worship.

Israel Davidson

Then there was Professor Israel Davidson, a very meticulous scholar. In his four-volume *Thesaurus of Medieval Hebrew Poetry* was collected nearly all that was extant of the works of the poets of the synagogue during a period of a thousand years, together with whatever information was available about the authors and the times and places in which they lived. Thanks to his explanations, the prayers of the synagogue, in the various rituals, became a fascinating subject of study.

For the study of the Bible, no replacement had, in the first year of my internship as a student at the seminary, as yet been found for the recently martyred Professor Israel Friedlander, who in addition to his expertise in the Hebrew Scriptures was also an outstanding Arabist. It was only later that Professor Hoschander was secured from Dropsie College in Philadelphia to fill that post.

Hyamson, Levin, and Kaplan

Codes were taught by Rabbi Moses Hyamson, whom the Orach Chayim Synagogue, a fortress of German Orthodoxy in New York, had brought over from London, where he had long served as the dayan, or rabbinical judge, of the United Hebrew Synagogues. The great value of the instruction of this lovable, although absent-minded, mentor lay in the practical advice he gave to prospective rabbis for the solution of ritual problems that might be presented to them by members of their flocks.

A few hours a week were devoted to the reading of modern Hebrew literature. Professor Morris Levin was in charge of this department. He was an inspiring teacher. However, the most stimulating of all my guides and mentors, who made his pupils think by the questions he aroused in their minds, was Professor Mordecai M. Kaplan. Himself a graduate of the seminary, he had been appointed by Dr. Solomon Schechter, the president of the seminary, to head the Teacher's Institute, which was attached to the rabbinical school.

In 1916 he founded the first synagogue center in America, known as the Jewish Center. He resigned from that institution in the year in which I entered the seminary on account of the differences that had arisen between himself and the lay leaders of his congregation on account of his unorthodox religious views. A year later he organized the Society for the Advancement of Judaism, with a synagogue of its own, in which its spiritual leader's innovations in Jewish religious theory as well as practice, as they developed, were put into operation.

I could not go along with Professor Kaplan in his Reconstructionist philosophy of Judaism. Neither could Professor Ginsberg, between whom and Professor Kaplan very sharp clashes often took place. Yet I learned a great deal from Professor Kaplan's critique of the various interpretations of the Jewish religion, much of which I felt was justified.

Unfortunately, the panaceas he prescribed for Jewry's ailments did not seem to me to provide the therapy for the maladies they were intended to cure. Most of all, however, did I profit from his analysis of the texts of the Midrashim, which I studied under his direction and guidance and in which his psychological approach proved to be extremely fruitful.

XIV

Four Fruitful Years

THE FOUR YEARS I SPENT at the Seminary were unquestionably the intellectually most productive and spiritually most satisfying of my entire career. I drank thirstily at this inexhaustible fountain of Jewish knowledge, absorbing avidly and with relish every word that emanated from the mouths of my teachers. The notes I took, in my own shorthand that I developed, were so phonetically accurate that they recorded even the mispronunciations, due to the fact that some of the professors, not being natives of the United States, were unable to articulate correctly some of the sounds of the English language as spoken by Americans. This sometimes led to comical results.

German Accent

Thus, for example, dear Professor Marx, though he had been in America nearly two decades, had during all that time been unable, like others who immigrated to this country when they were already adults, to rid himself of his heavy German accent. He had difficulty in particular in making the *th* sound which always came out as an *s*.

One day he lectured on a certain period in medieval Spanish Jewish history. He mentioned the name of a king that sounded in my ears like Alfonsi Levins. But for the life of me I could not understand how a Spanish ruler could have been given an appellative with an ending such as that of Alfonsi. Even more mystifying was the surname of Levins. Not until I looked up the reference in a history textbook did I discover that the person referred to was Alfonso, whom Dr. Marx had called Alphonse, as in French, and that what I had taken down as "Levins" was really "the eleventh."

"Faith" not "Face"

On another occasion, Professor Marx spoke of a Jew who had changed his "face," and I had the impression at first that he had plastic surgery performed which produced a change in his physiognomy. Then I learned that it was the conversion of the individual in question from Judaism to Christianity that was meant, and that he had changed his "faith," not his "face."

This same Professor Marx, who was always present at the Sabbath morning services held at the seminary when it was still located in the modest three-story building on 123rd Street between Amsterdam Avenue and Broadway, would invariably fall asleep at the moment when a student preacher would deliver his practice sermon, and always managed to wake up just when the discourse was concluded. Apparently the talks of the novices, from which he rarely could learn anything that might be of interest, were so boring to this learned man, that he could not keep his eyes open while they went on. One of our comrades, who was a bit of a rogue, thought up a scheme whereby he might rouse the professor from this habitual somnolescence. He chose as an illustration for the point he was going to make an episode in the life of Alexander the Great. When he came to the words: "The reign of *Alexander marks* the beginning of a new era in history," the good man, hearing his name called, shook himself awake from his slumber, and the audience had a good laugh.

If there were other members of the seminary faculty of whose idiosyncracies the pranksters among the students were occasionally tempted to take advantage for their personal amusement, Professor Kaplan was not one of them. If any one of his pupils ever had the temerity to irritate him, he was quickly made to feel the fury of this teacher's wrath and dissuaded forever from repeating his error. There was no toleration of nonsense in Dr. Kaplan's class. The rabbinate, for which his pupils were supposed to be preparing, was too serious a profession to allow for such frivolities.

Boaz Cohen

Among the older students at the seminary to whom I was especially attracted was Boaz Cohen. A native of Bridgeport, Connecticut, he had entered the rabbinical school a year before me. He impressed me deeply by his knowledge of the Talmud, which was quite unusual at that time for a young man who was not a product of the East European yeshivot.

After his graduation from the seminary, he joined its faculty as instructor in Talmud. Years later, upon the passing of Professor Hyamson, who was close to ninety at his death, Boaz Cohen was appointed professor of codes. For a long time he headed the Bet Din of the Rabbinical Assembly. While he served as chairman of its Law Committee, no decision was issued that was not fully in keeping with the Halakah.

Boaz Cohen was also well acquainted with the works of Juedische Wissenschaft, the scientific and critical study of the Jewish past and Judaism's traditional literature that originated in nineteenth-century Germany. Most of these books were then written in German. It was because of the desire that my conversations with him aroused in me to build a library of my own, concentrating on these subjects, that I concurred readily in his proposal that we spend the four months of our summer vacation in Europe, particularly in Berlin, where several of his friends were then pursuing graduate studies in the famous seats of learning located in that city.

I was in a position financially to undertake such a journey without asking my father for assistance. Between private lessons I had given to the Politziner boys to prepare them for their Bar Mitzvah and the prizes I had collected at the seminary, where tuition was free, I had managed in two years to accumulate a total of twelve hundred dollars. This was more than ample to pay for my passage, second class, from New York to Hamburg and back, for railway fare, hotels, sightseeing, the purchase of books, and even the manufacture of several suits of clothing. Mr. Leo Ornstein, a friend of our family and a member of my father's choir in Hamburg, and an excellent tailor besides, made them for me.

For fear that they might refuse to give their consent, I did not consult my parents about the matter. But after I had purchased my steamship tickets, I confronted them with a fait accompli. By then, of course, it was too late for them to object. Besides, I was already twenty years of age, old enough to be able to take care of myself. Furthermore, I would have an opportunity to visit my maternal grandfather, Yidel Kaufman, the revered shochet (ritual slaughterer, next in rank, in the Jewish ecclesiastical hierarchy, to a rabbi) of my mother's native town of Brzesko, and other relatives.

So, with the blessing of both my father and mother and their admonition not to expose myself to danger, I left, shortly after the conclusion of the school year, for Europe. The trip was to last sixteen weeks, in the course of which I toured no less than eight countries.

XV
Touring Europe

OUR FIRST STOP after landing in Hamburg was Holland. Having managed to maintain their neutrality during the first world conflict, the Dutch Netherlands had escaped the ravages of war. It was thither that Emperor Wilhelm II retired after the defeat of Germany, which had started the bloody contest in which most of the countries of Europe as well as the United States were to become involved.

As a starter, I got off at the town of Groningen in the north of Holland, a city of about 100,000 inhabitants with a Jewish population of around 2,500. The reason was that my father's younger brother was the cantor of the one and only synagogue maintained by the small Jewish community, which consisted for the most part of natives of Holland.

Uncle Levi

Uncle Levi, who externally bore a striking likeness to my father, but was neither as talented nor as worldly, did not seem too happy with his position. The salary was small, hardly sufficient to maintain a family, including a wife and six children. The members of his congregation possessed neither the Jewish learning nor the piety that he would have wanted them to have. He was far from enamored with the guttural language which was their vernacular. He looked for a change and his quest was rewarded when, a year later, he received a bid, with the help of my father, to fill the post of cantor that had been vacated by my father eleven years earlier in Hamburg.

There was not much to keep me in Groningen outside of my relatives. The only museum was not prepossessing. The streets seemed to be poorly paved, and the buildings, with their tremendous doors and windows, old and run down, dating for the most part from the seventeenth century.

Glad to Leave

I was therefore glad, after a stay of a few days, to leave for the country's beautiful capital, the Hague, with its modern edifices, especially the Peace Palace, and its lovely parks and gardens, its shady trees, and the multitudes of flowers, notably roses and tulips, seen everywhere.

From the Hague, it was only a few miles to the popular sea resort of Scheveningen. That was where I had arranged to meet my friend Boaz Cohen. Sufficiently provided with specimens of the then "almighty" American dollar, which every European at that time was anxious to get a hold of, we checked in at the most luxurious of Scheveningen's hotels, the Kursaal (Casino), situated right on the beach overlooking the English Channel.

For one day we lived like royalty, sinking in the evening into the softest and downiest of featherbeds in a suite of rooms that were the lushest of the lush we had seen. All this was done at the equivalent of two dollars a day. But very soon came the pay-off.

In the afternoon of our second day in this lovely vacation spot, as we were walking along the Wandelhoofd (boardwalk), we heard a voice behind us saying, "Rosenblatt and Cohen, where are your passports?" We turned around and, being shown by our questioner his credentials as a police officer, presented to him our documents of identification. "Why didn't you tell the clerk at your hotel that you were Americans?" he continued. "Because," we replied, "he didn't ask us. All he wanted to know was where we came from, and we had just arrived from Hamburg."

Rates Quadrupled

The reason why the detective had been sent after us was that, although Boaz and I had conversed in German, in which both of us were fluent, Boaz had exploded in English when he became angry and lost his temper, since he didn't know enough German cuss-words. Someone among the hotel personnel must have overheard him and notified the police. Of course no charges were pressed against us because we had not denied our American nationality. However, when we looked at our bill upon our return to the hotel, we found that the rates had quadrupled. That was more than we could afford as students with a limited budget, and so we were compelled to transfer to more modest quarters.

From Holland we moved on to Berlin, Germany's number-one metropolis and the capital of what had been a mighty empire. One of the most beautiful cities in the world at that time, it seemed, since none of the battles had been fought on German soil and aerial bombardment was not yet in vogue, and despite the hardships that had been endured by the civilian population, virtually untouched by the war. Its palaces, museums, public buildings, universities, located on such famous thoroughfares as Unter den Linden, and its parks like the Tiergarten (zoo), with their statues and trees, were intact.

However, its currency had fallen to unprecedented depths. This made it an ideal place, for foreigners with dollars to spend, to shop in. I was able, for a mere bagatelle, to acquire such essentials in my field of studies as Levy's dictionary of the Talmud and the Midrash, which would have, in the United States, cost at least ten times what I paid for them in Germany.

On the morning of the Sabbath of our stay in Berlin, we worshipped at the Machzikei Hadass Synagogue, one of the strongholds of German Orthodoxy, of which Rabbi Meyer Hildesheimer was the spiritual leader. The sanctuary was filled to capacity. On Sunday we visited the Oranienburger Temple, the chief house of worship of the Reform community, in which the women were seated in a separate gallery as in Orthodox synagogues, the male worshippers all wore prayer shawls, and the praying was done exclusively in Hebrew. What made it a Reform temple was the fact that the organ was played on Saturdays and holidays, not by a Jewish but a gentile organist.

XVI

Germany and Poland

MY ITINERARY IN GERMANY included, in addition to Hamburg, where I was the guest of my old classmates the Wigderowitsches, such cities as Frankfort on the Main, Dresden, Breslau, and Munich. Because the arrangements for my lodging were made by my German friends in Frankfort, my hotel room there cost me the equivalent of less than a dollar in American currency. I attended a service in the Friedberger Anlage, the synagogue presided over by Dr. Solomon Breuer, the son-in-law of Rabbi Samson Raphael Hirsch, founder of German neo-Orthodoxy. It was a magnificent edifice in which, on an ordinary weekday morning, there assembled for prayer no less than four hundred worshippers.

Dresden Like Porcelain

Dresden resembled very much the porcelain bearing its name, which was produced there. In Breslau, the home of the first modern rabbinical seminary, the faculty of which boasted historians of the highest order like Heinrich Graetz, and talmudical scholars of the caliber of Zacharias Frankel, I was entertained by an old colleague of my father's, Cantor Altmann.

In Munich, the gay capital of Bavaria, I picked up, as I was walking on the street near the synagogue, a handbill bearing the legend: "Kill the Jews. They are our misfortune." This happened two years before Adolf Hitler's first abortive attempt to seize power. Naturally such expressions of hate were quite upsetting to the five thousand Jewish residents of Munich and made them uneasy. It did not seem to disturb the rest of the inhabitants, who went about their business as if nothing was wrong. While in Munich I visited several of the city's art galleries. I was also anxious to attend the performance of Wagner's *Parsifal* at the celebrated Prinz-Regenten Teater. However, tickets had been sold out in advance for weeks because, on account of the tailspin downward fall of the mark, people spent the money they earned as soon as they received it. In spite of the fact that I had been definitely informed that there was no chance of obtaining admission even for standing, I decided to try my luck.

On the trolley going in the direction of the opera house, I noticed a student twirling in hand what looked like a ticket. So I inquired of him how I could go about acquiring one. Whereupon he offered to sell me his for the price of eight American cents. "Are you sure you don't want it for yourself?" I asked. "No, I am glad to dispose of it." However, when I presented myself at the box office and was requested to show my passport, I was told that as an American I would have to add ninety-two cents above the price I had paid my young friend. I swallowed hard when I heard this. But it was still cheap at one dollar to listen to five hours of the finest music ever presented.

Since Boaz was not interested in going with me to Poland and Czechoslovakia, where I wanted to look up relatives on my father's as well as my mother's side, we parted company there and then. I proceeded to Cracow, the ancient capital of Galicia, where my mother's youngest brother, Samuel Kaufman, who had accompanied us to America, served as chief cantor. The synagogue in which he officiated was very old, dating back to the sixteenth century, the time of Rabbi Moses Isserles, the famous codifier and foremost religious authority in his day of Ashkenazic Jewry, after whom it was named.

Most of the homes in this Polish urban center of several hundred thousand, almost half of whose inhabitants were Jews, lacked the most basic sanitary facilities. The toilets, where they were available, were out of order, and the stench from the outhouses was almost unbearable. It is no wonder that as a result of these conditions, in addition to the lack of food during the war, many residents contracted tuberculosis and other such ailments.

Smothered with Kindness

My uncle, who was comparatively well off, because he had married a businesswoman, the daughter of fairly prosperous hardware dealers, received me very cordially with the same warm hospitality as my father's brother in Groningen. His wife literally smothered me with kindness by making me sleep under a heavy feather quilt at night and serving me her culinary delicacies. Most of the Jews of Cracow, having been deprived by the government of the traditional sources of livelihood, namely, the tobacco and liquor trades, were compelled to eke out a precarious living by dealing with securities or the fluctuating currencies.

The stock exchange was just black with them, and in order to stay within the law they would use code names to designate what they offered for sale. American dollars were referred to as *lokschen* ("noodles") and the tattered Polish zlotys as *shmates* ("rags").

Not far from Cracow was the town or village of Brzesko, known as Briegel to its Jewish inhabitants, where my mother was born. My maternal grandfather, the generally beloved shochet (ritual slaughterer) Idel Kaufman, was still living there. Then a man of eighty-four, he did not have a wrinkle in his face. I stayed in his modest one-story wooden frame house, and when I accompanied him to the steam bath on Friday afternoon, I noted how neat and tidy he was and that he had a skin as smooth as that of an infant. In his younger years, he had been accustomed to taking ablutions in the river every morning even in the cold winter days by breaking the ice. Notwithstanding his advanced age, he led all the prayers on the Day of Atonement and with real fervor. Because I was meticulous in the observance of the traditional precepts of Judaism, despite my Western garb, including a short jacket that I wore, he and his neighbors called me *Dus frimme Deitschel* ("the religious little German").

Extremely Poor

Having been informed that a sister of my father's, Aunt Yita Rubinfeld, lived in Wadowice, high up in the Carpathian Mountains, I took a train to that little place to look her up. I had time only for an overnight stay and was glad to be able to get away when I did. The family was extremely poor. Their living quarters, which consisted of two rooms in a slanting low-roof wooden house, lacked all comforts. In addition, I had a sudden stomach upset. Yet I was happy to have been able to spend with them the few hours I did because I had not wanted to slight them.

The capital of Greater Poland and its number-one metropolis was Warsaw. In size its Jewish community was second only to that of New York. It was a center of Jewish culture, publishing a number of Yiddish dailies and one in Hebrew. I was anxious to become acquainted with this city, whose Jews had been so prominent in Jewish history for more than a century. I was afforded an opportunity to satisfy this desire because my cousin Melech Kaufman, who had been engaged as cantor by a synagogue in Philadelphia, had asked me to help his fiancée, a resident of Cracow, secure her immigration visa from the American consul in Warsaw.

It was a most interesting but also saddening experience. Never before had I seen so much misery and its usual companion, filth. I could not get out fast enough from the overcrowded Jewish neighborhood—a sort of replica of the lower East Side in New York—such streets as Gensha and Nalewki, which figure so prominently in books like Hersey's *The Wall*. It was fortunate for me and Dobshu that we were able to obtain two rooms in the apartment of a German woman on the fashionable Yerusalemska Aleya. Otherwise I don't think I would have held out for the two days I had to spend in the city.

XVII

Slovakia and Westward

THE SLOVAK PORTION of Czechoslovakia lies directly south of Galicia. There, on the bank of the Danube River is situated Bratislava (Pressburg in German), the city in which I was born when my father served as its chief cantor. This was my destination upon leaving Poland. My recollection of what it looked like is rather vague.

All I am now able to remember is that I arrived on the eve of Tish'ah b'Av (the ninth of Ab, the anniversary of the destruction of the Temple of Jerusalem). I spent the next day fasting. I had a chance, at the services in my father's former synagogue to meet, among others, Rabbi Akiba Schreiber, whose father, the late Rabbi Simchah Bunim Schreiber, had held me at my initiation into the Covenant of Abraham. I recall furthermore that I was made rather uncomfortable during the two nights that I slept there by the indestructible Bratislava fleas, who attacked me in bed.

Duty Bound

Since I was so close to Trnava (Tyrnau), where my widowed Aunt Gittel, who had been so intensely jealous of my mother, lived with her family, I considered it my duty to visit her, and she did give me, her famous brother's son, a cordial reception. By the way, it was her son Josef, who had lost in a gamble twelve hundred dollars that my father had sent as a dowry for her youngest daughter, Nettie, so that it had to be replaced to the great chagrin of my mother.

I also went to visit my Aunt Feige Stauber in Verbo. It was in her learned husband, Ignaz, the ritual slaughterer and minister to all religious needs of the small Jewish community, that my mother often confided in her troubles, because he possessed, in addition to worldly wisdom, a great deal of common sense. One of his astounding feats was the writing, on a single postcard, of the entire Hebrew text of the Book of Esther.

His two daughters, who later became outstanding physicians, were liquidated by the Nazis. His son, Michael, managed to escape in time to Israel, but he had to give up his plans of a medical career, for which he had been preparing. He is at present a high official in Israel's internal revenue service.

Truncated Austria

From Bratislava it is only one hour's ride by trolley to Vienna. To this beautiful capital of the once proud and prosperous Austro-Hungarian empire, with its crazy quilt of ethnic groups, I was accompanied by Aunt Gittel's oldest daughter, Kreindel, who had stayed with us for a year in Hamburg prior to our departure to America.

Conditions in truncated Austria were even worse than they were in Germany. Vienna was very much down at the heels. Most of the houses were badly in need of painting and repair. Beggars were to be seen by the hundreds in the most fashionable streets. The Austrian currency had become so worthless that I needed an entire briefcase to carry the paper money that I received in exchange for ten American dollars. People were spending whatever cash they had on hand as soon as they got hold of it. If they were to hoard it, it would become worthless.

The result was that nearly everybody was on the go. The demand for railroad tickets was so great that unless one stood in line for a day in front of the ticket office, getting a seat on a train was out of the question.

Ticket Stand-In

In order to be in a position to continue my journey from Vienna to Zurich, Switzerland, I was forced to hire a man, who was out of work—and there were many of them in Vienna at that time—to stand for me and not only purchase a railroad ticket for me, but also reserve a seat. I sent him out on Friday. When I came to my hotel on Saturday morning after attending services in the massive and beautiful synagogue of the Turkish-Jewish community, my stand-in brought me a ticket on the express going directly to Zurich. Unfortunately, it was to leave that very afternoon, which made it impossible, of course, for me to use it. So I sent him back and all he could get for me on a train departing on Sunday was a ticket to the next large station but without a seat reservation.

Having no alternative, I took it, and dragging my luggage myself, because no porters were available, I stood in line. In order to obtain a place card I had to crash the line and I barely made it. To cut a long story short, my trip to Zurich took twenty-eight instead of eighteen hours. I changed from one local train to another eight times and had to stand up in most of the coaches. When I finally arrived in Zurich, I made a bee-line for the first hotel with a vacancy and lay down on my bed without undressing.

I was so exhausted that I felt that without at least a little nap I would be unable to carry on. It was six in the afternoon when I went to sleep with the sun still shining brightly. When I awoke, I noted that it was seven o'clock. However, it was not seven in the afternoon, but of the next morning. In other words, I had slept for thirteen whole hours without being aware of the lapse of time.

Swiss Sunrise

My ten-day vacation in Switzerland was delightful. Most of it was spent in Lucerne, that jewel among the cities of this land-locked little mountainous country of banks and clocks and chocolate, situated on the shores of Lake Lucerne and not far from the Rigi Peak. I boated on the lake, almost froze during the night spent on top of Mount Rigi to be ready to watch the sun rise out of the night at dawn, and took my meals at Restaurant Rosenblatt. The food was wholesome but not nearly as appetizing as the schnitzel or pastry I had eaten in Vienna.

My destination after Switzerland was Paris. My reaction to the pleasure capital of the world was love at first sight. I was completely captivated by all the beauty it had to offer to the eye of the beholder—its palaces, museums, public buildings, its famous thoroughfares, such as the Champs Elysées, Rue de Rivoli, and Rue de la Paix, the arches and bridges, the opera and other theaters and music halls. I took in all I was able to crowd into a ten-day sojourn, including visits to the Louvre, the palace of the Bourbons in Versailles, and the retreat of Napoleon at Fontainebleau.

Because of my adherence to the Jewish dietary laws, I was restricted to what French cooking I could taste at Dardek's, the only restaurant under rabbinical supervision, located in the same courtyard as the Rue Cadet Synagogue, where my father-in-law-to-be used to worship. Its first spiritual leader, Rabbi Weiskopf, who had died at the ripe age of

101, had the distinction of having held his position for seventy-eight years, a record indeed in the entire history of the rabbinate.

London Seemed Drab

Compared to Paris and its sunshine, London, with its usually overcast sky, even when it was not raining, seemed dull and drab, notwithstanding the large number of places of interest, such as the Houses of Parliament, the Tower of London, the British Museum, Buckingham Palace, and others which I would not have missed for anything. What struck me particularly during my stay there at that time were the enormous breakfasts served in the early morning hours, which contrasted sharply with the meager continental fare of chocolate and rolls. I was also amused by the sight of a man, clad in a cutaway, striped trousers, and high hat wheeling a bicycle with the tails flying in the wind.

XVIII

Columbia University

I RETURNED HOME just before the High Holidays, rich in experiences and accompanied by the nucleus of a library of basic Judaica, in which there figured such out-of-print classics as Solomon Munk's edition of the original Arabic text of the *Guide* of Moses Maimonides, and his excellent French translation. It was in a Paris bookstore that I acquired this specimen of nineteenth-century Jewish scholarship, which had been produced by its author when he was totally blind.

Columbia University

I had decided, when I entered the seminary, that I would take advantage of the arrangements made with Columbia University that would permit students of the seminary to pursue studies in the graduate departments of that institution of higher learning, the chief building complex of which was located only a few blocks from the seminary headquarters. So I enrolled in the department of Semitic languages, which was headed by Professor Richard Gottheil, the son of Dr. Gustav Gottheil, one of the early rabbis of New York's Temple Emanuel. Four days a week, from Monday to Thursday, immediately upon the conclusion of classes at the seminary, after gulping down whatever lunch I had brought along from home, I would run up the hill to Columbia to take my courses first in Arabic and Syriac and later on in Assyrian, Ethiopic, Middle Persian, and philosophy.

Among my classmates were, in addition to Boaz Cohen, people like Ralph Marcus, an outstanding Greek scholar, and Abraham Halkin, who was destined to become a first-class Arabist, as well as Rabbi

Harry Halpern, a successful and witty member of the rabbinate. Boaz often needled Professor Gottheil, whose memory had begun to fail him, by correcting the mistakes our teacher had made. I was much more discrete in such situations. The result was that when the opportunity presented itself for the appointment of a lecturer in Semitics at Columbia, it was awarded to me. Only afterwards did the good professor learn that I was the son of a celebrity like Cantor Josef Rosenblatt.

The knowledge I acquired at Columbia University was as satisfying and stimulating as the intellectual nurture I received at the seminary. I quickly mastered the elements of Arabic, which was the language in which the classical works of medieval Jewish philosophy were written, and Syriac, which was virtually identical with the Aramaic of the Talmud. Assyrian, on account of its thousands of symbols, representing syllables, and Ethiopic, in which consonants and vowels are combined, were more difficult. As for Middle Persian (Pahlavi), the Persian of the talmudic era, I never went beyond nibbling at it.

Each of my mentors, Professors Gottheil, Kraeling, and Jackson, was, in his respective field, a rather competent guide. But if I attained the proficiency I did in Judeo-Arabic literature, it was because it was my good fortune that, during my second year in Columbia, Dr. David Yellin of Jerusalem had been invited to give the courses in Arabic for a two-year period. It was he who introduced me to the Koran and its commentaries. It was under him that I read Arabic prose and poetry. By listening to him, a native of the Middle East, I learned to do what is so difficult for the average Occidental, namely, to articulate correctly the sounds of Arabic consonants. By the way, Dr. Yellin's Hebrew was as mellifluous as his Arabic. He was a first-class educator, and it is quite fitting that the Teachers' Seminary in Jerusalem, which had been founded by him, was named after him.

Dull Lecturer

The most eminent and internationally renowned of the members of the faculty of philosophy of Columbia University, at whose feet it was my privilege to sit, was unquestionably Professor John Dewey. The most original thinker produced by America, his distinctive contribution to human thought was his theory of pragmatism. By giving priority to action over belief, he came close to the view predominant in Jewish thinking.

However, for all the impact made by his writings, particularly in the field of education, Professor Dewey was one of the dullest lecturers I had ever encountered. Since his class began right after the lunch period, it was hard for the listeners to keep awake as he droned on and on in an expressionless voice, looking out absentmindedly through the window, his socks rolling over his shoes. One Chinese student, who had his seat directly in front of him, would invariably snore out loud during the most involved portion of the lecture. But the professor was so completely lost in thought that he never noticed it.

When I began my rabbinical studies at the seminary, my father was at the height of his powers as a chazan and concertist. His recordings, which spread his fame all over the world, brought him a handsome revenue. He was in great demand as a cantor, and he received for his appearances on the concert stage the largest fees ever paid to members of his profession.

But just as his sun of prosperity began to shine and he could afford to live a life of affluence and become, in addition thereto, because of his inclination as well as his influence, a patron of the talented and a benefactor of countless Chassidic rabbis, Satan entered to spoil it all and lead to his material ruin. The story of his involvement with the ill-fated *Light of Israel*, the plea of bankruptcy which he was compelled to file in January of the year 1925, and his entrance into vaudeville to earn enough money to pay back his creditors, is related in full detail in my biography of him published in 1954. I can, therefore, dispense with repeating it now.

XIX

Rabbi, Preacher, and Teacher

MY FATHER'S FINANCIAL difficulties made me all the more eager to become economically independent as soon as possible. This was an added reason for my devoting myself most earnestly to my studies so as to be in a position to earn my livelihood without applying to him for support. Truth to tell I had always refrained, when I was in a position to avoid it, from imposing burdens upon him. Whereas my brother Leo and my sister Nettie enrolled in Columbia and New York Universities for their college education, I was perfectly satisfied to obtain mine at City College, which then made no tuition charge, yet had a high academic standing.

My rabbinical training at the seminary as well as the residence requirements for the doctorate at Columbia were also gratis. I was able to pay for my clothes and the books I needed out of the fees for officiating on the High Holidays in Philadelphia, Arverne, Detroit, and Chicago, being sent always to synagogues in which services were conducted in a strictly Orthodox manner. My income was further augmented by the prizes awarded me every year by the seminary for outstanding scholarship.

I had long set my heart, upon my graduation from the seminary, to augment my rabbinical education by a year of intensive study of the codes of Jewish law at one of the yeshivot in the Land of Israel and receive, from the rabbinical authorities of the Holy Land, the traditional ordination, or semichah.

An opportunity to realize this wish presented itself to me quite by accident. At the beginning of my last semester at Columbia University, a non-Jewish classmate informed me about the availability of a fellowship at the American School of Oriental Research in Jerusalem. This would make it possible for me to spend, if I would be lucky enough to obtain it, an entire school year at that institution and take advantage, during my sojourn in the most revered center of Jewry, of whatever else it might have to offer for my intellectual enrichment. The information had no sooner been divulged to me, than I made application, through Professor Marx, for admission to the necessary preliminary examinations.

While preparing for my finals at the seminary—and for the one in Talmud alone I crammed for three days and three nights with only four hours of sleep a day in twenty-four—I also reviewed the grammars of five Semitic languages, Latin and Greek, and the history and geography of Palestine. I took my tests but gave the matter no further thought, both because I was too busy and also because I assumed that the chances of winning the award were very remote. However, on the second day of Passover a letter arrived from Professor Montgomery of Yale University, the authority on the Samaritans, notifying me of being the winner.

Overwhelming

Needless to say, my joy at this unexpected news, was overwhelming. The stipend of one thousand dollars provided by the Hazard Fellowship, plus five hundred that I would earn by preaching at the Shaarey Tefilah Synagogue of Far Rockaway on the High Holidays, was ample not only to pay for my passage to and from Palestine but also for all the expenses of my stay of ten months in Jerusalem.

I came through my finals at the seminary with flying colors achieving an average of over ninety-eight. It was particularly gratifying to learn that I had scored a perfect mark with Professor Ginzberg, who had the reputation of being a hard taskmaster. My graduation, which my parents were unable to attend because of my father's vaudeville engagements in the Far West, took place on the first Sunday in June.

The day before was, as I recall it, one of the hottest days of the year. It was the custom for the graduates to be invited on the Sabbath preceding the commencement for lunch at the home of Professor Ginzberg. The walk of a mile and a half, from the seminary up the hill to the apartment of the Ginzbergs in Washington Heights, in the blazing midday sun clad in a cutaway, was most uncomfortable. I was all perspiration upon reaching my destination and drank so much ice-water that the next day I suffered severe stomach cramps. Under such conditions, to sit through the commencement exercises, in the course of which I was called up several times to collect prizes, was a veritable ordeal. How I managed to do it is still a mystery to me today. The fact is that I survived and walked off the platform crowned with the title of "Rabbi, Teacher, and Preacher in Israel," with distinction and at the head of my class in scholarship.

XX

Courting Claire

NOW THAT MY FORMAL preparation for a career that would make me self-sustaining was over, the time had come to look for a companion and partner who would be willing to share with me life and fortune. It had certainly never been my intention to remain a bachelor. Furthermore, even though prior to my graduation the acquisition of the knowledge that would qualify me to fill a rabbinical post had been my sole and exclusive occupation, I was fully aware of the fact that the rabbinate included important social functions. A man cannot minister effectively to the needs of his flock unless he is able to associate himself with them in weal and woe. In the performance of these tasks, the assistance of real helpmeet is not only invaluable. It is indispensable, as was proven to me later.

Where would I find such a woman, who would become, if not my alter ego—one scholar in the family was enough—at least my complement, rounding out, as it were, my personality? If I had not previously attempted to face this problem, it was because I did not consider it fair to become too much involved emotionally with the person who was to be closer to me than any other being on earth before I was in a position to carry out all my obligations as a husband. Now, at last, I had reached the point where I thought I could.

Fortunately for me I did not have to search far and wide. As the contemporary and friend of my oldest sister, Nettie, Claire Woloch had been a frequent visitor at our home for several years before I decided actively to woo her. She seemed to me to possess the qualifications I looked for, all the virtues that would make her eligible as a future rabbi's wife. She was not only attractive. She was positively beautiful. Always dressed in good taste, she was intelligent, dependable, outgoing, and warm. She liked people, and their company. She enjoyed good music, literature, and art. She listened to enlightening lectures with a critical ear.

She was, in addition, reared in a home in which the time-honored traditions of Judaism, such as the observance of the Sabbath and the festivals and the Jewish dietary laws, were combined with modern culture. What was particularly encouraging to me, so far as she was concerned, was that my mother, whose opinion I valued greatly, too was very fond of her. The blessings she held in prospect far exceeded in value the most opulent dowry. And so petite Claire Woloch became my choice.

Lacked Technique

But how was I to go about the matter of winning her by convincing her that she was my destined one? Having spent nearly all my waking hours on books, I was not too well versed in "the way of a man with a maid." My brother-in-law Nathan remarked I lacked the technique. Luckily my younger brother Leo, the Beau Brummel of the family, who had long been courting his Doris, a fifth-or sixth-generation Jewish American, came to my assistance. He arranged to have Claire invited to our summer home in Long Branch for a few weeks, and then things took their anticipated course. I had a chance to take walks with Claire alone.

I liked to go canoeing, so we tried that on the lake. Unfortunately a storm arose at the end of the first outing and we nearly drowned. Finally I plucked up enough courage to ask the crucial question. Her initial response was that there was much in me that she admired. Yet she was hesitant. The rabbinate, she said, made many personal demands. Was a man accustomed to locking himself in the ivory tower of scholarship capable of meeting such a challenge? A rabbi is always on display. He does not have much of a private life.

Many of my classmates, who envied me my scholastic achievements, also wondered how successful I would be in my chosen profession. So her first reaction was one of doubt. Furthermore, she could not forget my gaucherie in not inviting her directly to the seminary commencement but handing the invitation card, intended for her, to her parents, who, by their attendance, made up for the absence of my own father and mother. "If he wanted me to be there why didn't he ask me in person?"

She didn't realize, of course, that it was my shyness that was responsible for this faux pas.

Engaged

I was very unhappy because of this apparent rejection. However, fate, in the person of her father, was again on my side. It was he, who convinced her that for all its drawbacks life with a rabbi had its compensations. He thus prevailed on her to give her consent when I refused to accept her reluctance. And so we became engaged—Leo, too, now felt free to announce his engagement to Doris Podoll, and not long after Nettie became affianced to Harry Reiss, who had been asking for her hand prior to my courting Claire.

If I could have had my way, I would have married Claire without delay lest I lose her to somebody else who might find her as desirable as she seemed to me. However, to schedule the wedding for that summer would have been neither practical nor feasible. First of all there was that Hazard Fellowship I had just won, with the many opportunities it offered, not only for the continuation for an entire year of my Semitic studies at the American School of Oriental Research in Jerusalem, but also for courses at the recently opened Hebrew University. In addition, I looked forward to attending classes at the rabbinical school founded by the Land of Israel's first chief rabbi, Abraham Isaac Kook, from whom I hoped to obtain, once I had satisfied the requirements, the much coveted traditional ordination, or Semichah.

It would hardly have been possible to give undivided attention to all the taxing disciplines I had to master while being burdened with the chores of setting up a household and devoting time to a newly wedded bride. But even once these problems were satisfactorily resolved, it would still have been necessary for either Claire's or my own father to subsidize her passage and provide for her board and lodging for the duration of our stay abroad. Neither of them was then in a position to do this.

Prudence, which is the better part of valor, counseled that I proceed to my destination alone, leaving Claire behind, trying though the separation might be for the period of at least ten months, and postpone the date of our nuptials to after my return. So on the day immediately following Yom Kippur I set out on my journey. Traveling by land and sea, with but a short stopover in Paris during the intervening days of Sukkot, I arrived two weeks later in Jerusalem.

Samuel Rosenblatt at age 23, time of graduation from the Seminary

Samuel Rosenblatt in Palestine at age 24

XXI

Hazard Fellow

THE ASCENT VIA TRAIN up the rugged mountains surrounding Jerusalem was as inspiring as it was breathtaking. Very soon, I said to myself as I was approaching the outskirts of the holy city, I will be able to record in the words of the psalmist: "My feet have been standing in thy gates, O Jerusalem." Although it was mid-October, according to the calendar, the sun was even in the late afternoon still so bright as to be almost blinding.

Because it had not rained for fully half a year since spring, the roads were dusty. All vegetation had dried up. There was not a blade of grass to be seen anywhere, and shade-giving trees were few and far between. Yet the air at the altitude of three thousand feet above sea-level was pure and fresh and bracing, and there was something solid about the one- and two-story white sandstone houses of Arab architecture, with their small arched windows and their vaulted ceilings that gave shelter to the residents within from the heat of the tropical sun without.

I became enamored of Jerusalem from the moment I laid eyes on it. What impressed me was the uniqueness of its character, the many historic landmarks found within its boundaries, which brought back memories of its chequered past, as well as the varied panorama of its hills and valleys.

The Hotel Warshawsky was my headquarters in Jerusalem from the time of my arrival until my room was ready for me at the recently completed edifies of the American School of Oriental Research. It was anything but a luxury hotel. It lacked running water and modern plumbing. The walls as well as the floors and ceiling were of stone. The furniture was primitive. Illumination was by kerosene lamps. But it was clean. The beds were comfortable. The food, though different from what I was accustomed to at home, was adequate; and since I was not a fastidious eater anyhow, I had no complaints during the few days of my stay there.

Anyhow, it was about the best in hostelry available at the time in Jerusalem. Besides, it gave me the opportunity to come in contact with at least two celebrities of world renown who frequented the place. One was the Hebrew poet laureate, Chaim Nachman Bialik. A squat, medium-sized man in his fifties, he was, notwithstanding his fame and popularity, a modest and most approachable person. He was everybody's friend and beloved by nearly all strata of Palestinian Jewish society. "About Bialik," he used to say of himself, parodying a talmudic expression "no one disagrees." *Bialik les man depalig.*

Upon his return from a visit to the United States, where he had been very much wined and dined, he remarked jokingly, because of the many chicken dinners he had to attend, that in America Zionism seems to be standing on chicken's feet. After his death in the year 1934, the city of Tel Aviv converted the home that had been built for him into a Bialik museum.

Another Jewish great whom I met at the Hotel Warshawsky was Henrietta Szold, the founder of Hadassah. A little whisp of a woman in her middle sixties, with graying hair, she was, in spite of being rather strong-willed, kind and down to earth. For all her accomplishments, which were already then numerous, she did not disdain discussing, as with an equal, with a twenty-three-year-old graduate of a rabbinical seminary, Jewish and world problems. I felt deeply flattered by this compliment. Meekness seems to be an attribute of the truly distinguished.

This truth was again demonstrated to me when I was ushered a few days later into the presence of William Foxwell Albright, the director at the time of the American School of Oriental Research in Jerusalem. He had already then won a reputation as one of the world's leading biblical archaeologists, conversant with all the languages of the ancient Middle East, although he was only thirty-four years old. Tall, lean, and with balding blond hair, he towered above my five-foot four inches. Yet he made me feel so much at ease with him. So, too, did his wife, Ruth. Though she boasted in her own right a Ph.D. in Sanskrit, her air, when she spoke to me, was that of an ordinary housewife.

Both of them, he a faithful Methodist and she a former Episcopalian, turned, since her settlement in the Holy Land, into a devout Catholic, respected my religious beliefs as well as my observance of the tenets of Judaism, about which they were were better informed than many Jews. Never, during the close to half a century of my association with them, did I have reason to doubt the genuineness of the goodwill, friendship, and esteem they evinced toward me and Claire.

The American School

The buildings of the American School in Jerusalem were the most modern and up-to-date in the Holy City. While they lacked electricity and central heating in the year 1925, and whoever wanted to take a hot bath once a week had to put in his order a few days in advance, the bedrooms were provided with showers and the windows had screens, which did not, however, prevent the tiny gnats from slipping through the openings, and were they mean!

The spirit of a true fraternity of learning prevailed in this American archaeological center. Scholars of various races and representing sundry denominations mingled freely with each other. Protestant ministers, teachers and students of the Dominican Seminary across the street, Mohammedan divines, and Jewish rabbis like myself engaged in animated discussions revolving for the most part about the meaning of passages in the Bible, which constituted the chief subject of interest.

It was a real cosmopolitan atmosphere, in which a varied assortment of languages were spoken—German, English, French, Arabic, and Hebrew. Since the Albrights had a German maid and a Christian Arab houseboy, their two-year-old son would form sentences consisting of a mixture of English, German, and Arabic, such as "Gib mir a little Moye" ("give me a little water").

I would have my breakfast, which consisted almost invariably of cereal, milk, and medium-boiled eggs, in the dining room of the school, which was my home for nearly ten months. Lunch and dinner I ate at a boarding house maintained by Mrs. Friedman, an attractive Jewish American widow in her thirties. Among my fellow residents at the American School were Sheldon Blank, Jacob Marcus, and Nelson Glueck, all of them fledglings of Hebrew Union College, the rabbinical school of Reform Jewry in America.

Of these the first knew hardly any Hebrew at all upon his arrival. He now teaches Bible at his alma mater. The second became the outstanding authority on American Jewish history, and the last one of the foremost archaeologists of Palestine, and during the last decade of his life president of Hebrew Union College. At the home of Mrs. Friedman, I met Jews from every part of the globe. There was among them a Sephardi from Greece, with whom I conversed in Ladino.

Another, Dr. Malchi, was a physician in the employ of the British mandatory government. He had just had a run-in with the inmates of an Arab hostel where there had been an outbreak of typhus. When, as a precautionary measure, he issued an order for all the boarders to shower, such a howl was raised that it almost cost him his job.

Then there was a Mr. Rabinowitz from Russia. When one of the guests from Germany at the conclusion of the meal got up and exclaimed, "Mahlzeit" ("blessed meal"), the Russian not to be outdone by him in politeness, bowed in return, saying "Rabinowitz."

My first duty as Hazard fellow at the American School of Oriental Research was to put the books on the shelves of the library and arrange them according to subjects, in alphabetical order. Once this task was completed I had time to read, under the direction of Dr. Albright, when he was not away on his archaeological expeditions, on a few of which I accompanied him, North Semitic inscriptions of Hebrew and Aramaic texts written in Phoenician characters as well as Egyptian hieroglyphics.

I also enrolled as a student of Arabic at the Hebrew University. Classes were held by Professor Joseph Horovitz, the son of a rabbi in Frankfort on the Main, in an old Arab villa on top of Mount Scopus, where the first units of the Hebrew University were being erected.

XXII

A Year in Jerusalem

ONE OF MY CLASSMATES was Walter Fischel. Several years later he was made the head of the Department of Semitics of the University of California. His forte was the history of Jews in Moslem countries. S. D. Goitein was another one of my colleagues. He later taught Arabic at the Hebrew University as well as the University of Pennsylvania. A third was Issachar Joel, the editor in the original Judeo-Arabic of such Jewish philosophical classics as the *Guide of the Perplexed* of Moses Maimonides.

A fourth was Hartwig Baneth, one of the most meticulous scholars I ever encountered, and subsequently librarian of the university. All these fellow students hailed from Germany. Since Professor Horovitz was not yet fluent in Hebrew, he assigned to me the chore of translating, for the benefit of the Hebrew-speaking members of the class, his German rendering of the Arabic texts he had selected for his pupils' exercises.

In addition to this course I also took one in Septuagint Greek with Professor Schwabe. His classes were held at night. One evening, in midwinter, the rain, which was usually accompanied by wind, beat down with such fury that I was almost swept off balance as I went downhill on the winding road leading from Mount Scopus. Luckily for me I was covered from head to toe in raincoat, hood, leggings, and rubber-shoes, so that I reached my destination in safety, remaining completely dry underneath.

With these disciplines and the scouring of the contents of the Goldziher Library, which the university had just acquired for materials for my doctor's dissertation, I had enough to do to keep me busy and out of mischief. However, most of my waking hours were devoted to the study of the tractate Hullin of the Babylonian Talmud, and the works of the codifiers bearing on the Jewish dietary laws in order to qualify for semichah.

A friend of my father's, Dr. Burstein of New York, who was an intimate of Chief Rabbi Kook, had arranged for my admission as a student in his rabbinical school, then known as Mercaz Harav. A companion was assigned to me, first a young man by the name of Isaac Schulsinger and, when he became ill, Jacob Finkelstein. For nine months without interruption, I traversed for six days out of seven every week the distance of half a mile from the American School via Meah Shearim to the yeshivah, which was located on the second floor of a two-story house on the Street of the Prophet Elijah. It consisted of a main auditorium, which served as synagogue and house of study, and the apartment of the head of the institution.

At the end of the school year I presented myself at the home of Rabbi Samson Aaron Polonsky, a member of the official rabbinical court (Bet Din) of Jerusalem and a noted Jewish legal authority. After subjecting me to a thorough grilling on various aspects of rabbinic law and submitting a number of hypothetical problems for solution, he found me worthy of receiving the traditional ordination as an interpreter of Jewish religious law. I was similarly examined by the venerable Rabbi Jacob Moshe Charlap, an associate of the chief rabbi in the latter's rabbinical seminary. When these two qualified examiners had given their approval, the head of the rabbinate of the Holy Land affixed his signature to the document, which testified to my competence to serve as a rabbi in the traditional sense of umpire in matters of Jewish law.

Concentrated Study

Thus my weekdays from Sunday morning until Friday afternoon during the entire period of my sojourn in the Land of Israel were spent in concentrated study in three distinct areas, the American School of Oriental Research, the Hebrew University, and the yeshivah of Rabbi Kook. Each brought me in contact with a different world and a widely divergent school of thought.

The Sabbath, beginning with Friday evening, was, of course, a day of rest. I usually worshipped in the Yeshurun Synagogue, which was then still housed in a rented building. The congregation, which was the nearest approach to the modern Orthodoxy to which I was accustomed, was made up of doctors, lawyers and judges, professors of the Hebrew University, and businessmen, most of them immigrants from the United States, England, and Germany, with a few natives thrown in for good measure. The services were conducted by laymen who were able to chant the prayers.

I was often given the honor, once it became known whose son I was. So popular was my father's music in the Holy City that eight-year-old boys were glad to pay half a piaster (the equivalent of two and one-half cents) to hear a record of his played on a phonograph in a grocer's shop.

Occasionally, on Friday evenings I would visit the little prayer-rooms of the Chassidim in Meah Shearim. I also remember rising one Saturday morning before dawn to worship with the Yemenites, the swarthy little Jews from South Arabia, who would leave their shoes in front of the door before entering and squat on the floor or the benches all around the walls in the Turkish manner, swaying back and forth as they prayed in their peculiar sing-song.

It was there that I heard a Yemenite boy of about five recite the entire Song of Songs by heart in the distinctive Yemenite intonation. They always intrigued me, these Oriental coreligionists of mine, who seem to have come to us right out of the Middle Ages. Many of them possessed much Jewish learning, and all of them were industrious. I still recall vividly the spectacle that struck me one day, of a wiry, lean Yemenite Jew hauling an upright piano, tied to his back, up a steep hill.

On account of the water shortage that was prevalent in those days in Jerusalem, a bath was a luxury for most of its inhabitants. Yet for the sake of the Sabbath no Jew who took the holy day seriously would deny himself this luxury. It was a common sight on Friday afternoon for hundreds of elders to come out of the steam baths in Meah Shearim carrying towels under their arms and with beards dripping. These weekly ablutions must have contributed in no small measure toward their superior hygiene.

Because of my preoccupation with my studies, I had no time on weekdays for socializing. Only on the Sabbath was it possible for me to visit friends and acquaintances.

Among the homes to which I was often invited to spend a Friday evening was that of my former teacher, Professor David Yellin. The household of this gracious gentleman and scholar, who was a scion of an old Jersualem family in which the Sephardi and Ashkenazi strains were about evenly balanced, and of his equally hospitable wife, was a true "meeting place of the wise." One would encounter in its dining room, on the night of the Sabbath, professors of the Hebrew University like Dr. Moses Segal, the editor of the complete Hebrew text of the wisdom book of Ben Sira and an expert on Mishnaic Hebrew. Another frequent visitor was Rabbi Samuel Klein, on whose talmudic erudition Dr. Albright leaned heavily for the identification of Palestinian placenames.

Judges and government officials, Jewish as well as British, would drop in, among them the governor of Jerusalem, Sir Ronald Storrs. A suave Englishman whose polite manners bespoke the British aristocracy, he was underneath no friend of the Jews. Like the majority of the representatives of the mandatory power, he preferred the Arabs, who kowtowed to their overlords, to the brash sons of Israel, whose superior intelligence the second-rate appointees of his majesty's government, serving in Palestine, found it difficult to cope with.

Animated Conversation

One felt completely relaxed at the table of the Yellins. The conversation was animated and enlightening. There was a good bit of singing, in which I was able to show that I was a son of Yossele Rosenblatt. The refreshments were delicious.

Among the walks I would take on Saturday afternoons, one that is outstanding in my memory is the trip, in the company of Dr. Albright, to the home in Talpiot of the historian and publicist Dr. Joseph Klausner. What impressed me particularly was the fluent Hebrew spoken by the former in his conversation with our host, who was one of the foremost Hebrew men of letters of his generation and a prolific writer on Jewish history.

MOST OF MY TEN-MONTH SOJOURN in the Holy Land was spent in Jerusalem. I did, however, manage to take off about two weeks close to the time of Lag b'Omer for traveling through the country. I had a chance, during this fortnight, to visit Tel Aviv, which then had the freshness and cleanliness of a new settlement, with a population not exceeding thirty thousand. I stopped one night in a little four-room hotel in Balfouria. The owner was an immigrant from the United States. He had come to Palestine with nine unmarried daughters, all of whom found husbands. In America, he remarked, this could never have happened.

Palestinian Chicago

On the way to the Emek I passed through Afuleh, a little town in the wheat-growing belt, whose founders had hoped that it would develop some day into a Palestinian version of Chicago. This hope was, however, never realized.

In the rural settlement of Ein Charod I had an opportunity to observe at first hand what it was like to be a chalutz in those early pioneering days. At the time of my visit to that now-flourishing agricultural center, fully one-third of the inhabitants were down with malaria as a result of their draining of the mosquito-infested swamps. Meat was eaten only once a week on Shabbat. During the week the main midday meal consisted of soup, cucumbers, herring, and bread. Green vegetables were a rarity and fresh fruits a luxury item.

Yet the kibbutzniks of Ein Charod were considered prosperous compared with the members of such kibbutzim as Kibbutz Rodges of Hapoel Hamizrachi. The latter were still heavily in debt. They had decent shelters only for the cattle. And when it came to obtaining employment, they were, as constituents of the religious minority, often discriminated against, having to be satisfied with whatever jobs were left after the demands of the labor forces of the powerful nonreligious Histadrut had been filled.

From Ein Charod I journeyed to Haifa, where the old Technion building was then the chief landmark, and which had not yet grown beyond Hadar Hakarmel. A cousin of my father's by the name of Moshe Frankel, who had lived for a while in New York, had established a carbonated-drink factory there. At the northern end of the bay of Haifa lay the ancient town of Acre with its citadel and other relics from the age of the Crusaders. It had only a few Jewish inhabitants, one of them the proprietor of a match factory, who occasionally dined at my Pension Friedman.

My last stop was Safed. I stayed at the modest Arab house in which Claire's Aunt Pepi had her home. The very essence of human kindness, this childless sister of my future father-in-law led a very unhappy married life. She was most certainly not deserving of the treatment given her by her ne'er-do-well of a husband. Her efforts to make me feel comfortable during my short sojourn in her abode were simply indescribable. She died a few years later amidst very tragic circumstances, a victim of the Arab riots of 1929.

Before going to Safed I spent the evening of Lag b'Omer in nearby

Meron, the site of the tomb of the tannaitic sage Simon ben Yochai, the pupil of Rabbi Akiba and reputed author of the Zohar, the Bible of the mystics. Thousands of picnickers had converged on this hill-top town from all over the country. Jews of every sort and variety, young and old, modern and old-fashioned had come to participate in the Hilula, or merriment, in commemoration of Rabbi Simon son of Yochai. Chalutzim in shirts and shorts carrying on their shoulders Chassidim in long gabardines and wearing on their heads shtreimlach (beaver hats trimmed with foxtails), danced by the light of torches to the rhythm of the beating of drums and the thrum of guitars. As they did this they either chanted from the prayers of the synagogue or crooned Yiddish lullabies and songs of the new Palestine. Notwithstanding the great divergences between them, the participants proved by the way they made merry together that they were one people.

XXIII

Thinking of Claire and Home

IT WAS ALTOGETHER an eventful and busy year for me that ran by very quickly. Yet it did not go fast enough for a lonely bridegroom who was thinking constantly of his beautiful, young bride, six thousand miles away. I wrote to Claire almost every day, giving her a detailed account of my activities and experiences. She replied regularly. Her letters were always, as they still are today, interesting and vivid. I read them eagerly, hanging on every word, because they came from her hand.

Sometimes I missed her so much that I even proposed bringing her to Palestine, which was, of course, out of the question. Finally my time of waiting came to an end, and with the letters from the triumvirate of rabbis who granted me ordination in my pocket, and my term of study completed, I was able to return home.

On the way over I dropped into the Bodleian Library at Oxford University, England, in order to clear up certain passages in the photostat of the philosophical treatise of Abraham Maimonides that I had received from this institution at the seminary. The edition and translation of this still unpublished and hardly known magnum opus in Judeo-Arabic of the only son of Moses Maimonides had been suggested to me as the subject of a doctor's dissertation by my private tutor in Talmud, during my last two years as a student in the seminary, Dr. Gittelsohn, a product of the Lithuanian yeshivot, who had received his doctorate in Semitics in Berlin, Germany.

This matter having been taken care of, I was ready to sail for New York. However, before landing another item had to be attended to. Shortly after my arrival in Jerusalem I had decided, both because I did not want to be differentiated from my fellow students at the yeshivah of Rabbi Kook and on account of the limited water supply, to let my beard grow until it reached the length of my father's. Now, however, that I was about to see my intended again after a separation of ten months I was afraid that the sight of me with my overabundant hirsute adornment might shock her. So I set about trimming it. When I was met at the pier by my father and my father-in-law-to-be, this reduced size seemed still too much to suit what they believed to be Claire's taste. After all, the man whose proposal of marriage she had accepted was clean-shaven. She had not bargained for a full-bearded husband.

So as soon as I arrived home, and before they would let me face my bride, each took a pair of scissors in hand and started cutting. It must have been a most comical scene, the spectacle of these two elders, my father and my father-in-law-to-be, one on each side of me, trying out their tonsorial skill on their son and son-in-law. Unfortunately the results, when they were finished, were still not satisfactory, and so I was compelled to let a professional barber complete the job.

It was a glorious feeling to be back again in the company of my sweet, little bride. The fact that because of my father's recent bankruptcy our family was compelled to spend the hot summer months of this year in New York instead of moving to the seashore did not disturb us at all. Anyhow, it would have been rather inconvenient, since on the Sabbath after my homecoming, which happened to be Shabbat Nachamu, the Sabbath of Consolation following the Ninth of Ab, the Jewish Black Fast in commemoration of the destruction of the two Temples of Jerusalem, my youngest brother celebrated his Bar Mitzvah.

Like all of us Rosenblatt boys he read, in addition to the Haftarah (the message from the Prophets), the entire pentateuchal lesson. Father officiated as cantor, of course, accompanied by Machtenberg's choir, while I delivered the sermon. It was to be the last Sabbath service participated in by our family in the sanctuary of Ohab Zedek on 116th Street. The congregation had recently merged with one on West 95th Street. The synagogue located there was soon to become the headquarters of the joint community as the Jewish residents had begun to move out of Harlem, which was destined within less than a decade to become completely Judenrein.

XXIV

My First Position

ANOTHER REASON why it was at least to my personal advantage that we remained in New York was that I now had to look around seriously for a rabbinical position. I could certainly not contemplate marriage unless I was assured of a livelihood. But being placed was not too easy. For while pulpits were available, the number of vacancies in congregations that desired the services of an English-speaking rabbi, with a university training, and were Orthodox enough to meet my demands were rather scarce.

However, I did not have to wait too long, because one day in August, a friend of my father's, Rev. Asher Goldenberg, called up from Trenton, New Jersey, asking whether I could come to preach on the next Sabbath in the Adath Israel Synagogue of that city, which had just engaged him as its cantor. Upon learning that it was Conservative, I told him that I was not interested. However he persisted that I accept the invitation, because the congregation was new and there was a strong possibility of my persuading it to conform to my views.

Separate Seating

So "I went," and to use the phraseology of Julius Caesar, "Veni, Vidi, Vici—I came, I saw, I conquered." On Saturday night, immediately following the Friday evening on which I had delivered my trial sermon, I was informed by the president that I had been elected by the congregation as its rabbi.

"But what about the seating arrangements at services?" I asked.

"You know that one of my conditions is a separation of the sexes in keeping with the Orthodox tradition."

"This," they replied, "would be all right with us after the High Holidays. So far as this coming Rosh Hashanah and Yom Kippur are concerned, however, the seats have already been sold without such restrictions. We did it for the sake of our youth. But if after the holidays you could convince our young people to separate, we oldsters would raise no objection."

I remained adamant and was certain that the deal was off. But they did not give up.

"But we do want you. Can't you think of a plan that would make it possible for us to engage you without your having to compromise with your principles?" Well I did think of an arrangement, but it seemed so preposterous that I was sure it would be turned down. My proposal was to send them for the High Holidays a substitute to whom mixed seating was no object, and immediately thereafter I would take over and conduct the regular synagogue services according to my terms.

To my great surprise, they accepted the offer, and I thus became the first spiritual leader of the Adath Israel Congregation of Trenton, New Jersey at an annual salary of five thousand dollars, which was at that time pretty good compensation. It was certainly sufficient, together with what side income might accrue, to enable me to marry and set up a household. Just about that time the head of the department of Semitic languages at Columbia University, Professor Richard Gottheil, appointed me lecturer in Semitics at that institution of learning, and I was all set to fix the date of my wedding with Claire.

Ohab Zedek Synagogue
upper—116th Street, New York
lower—Norfolk Street, New York

The Rosenblatt Family at the time of Samuel's and Claire's marriage

XXV

Marriage

BECAUSE MY FATHER had to be on the West Coast early in October to fill his vaudeville commitments, our nuptials were scheduled for the Sunday immediately following the fall festival season, that is to say, after the three-day weekend of Shemini Atzeret, Simchat Torah, and Shabbat Bereshit.

The High Holidays of that year I had spent at home in Harlem. It was the last time I was to hear my father chant the prayers of Rosh Hashanah and Yom Kippur in his synagogue. For the first days of the Sukkot festival I went to Trenton to assume my rabbinical duties. On Shabbat Bereshit our entire family walked down to the 95th Street Synagogue, where I was called up to the Torah in honor of my impending marriage.

The marriage ceremony was held in the 116th Street sanctuary, which was filled to overflowing, while hundreds of people who were unable to get in stood outside. Among the members of the rabbinate who participated was Dr. Drachman, the American-born associate for many years of Dr. Philip Klein, who had died while I was in Palestine. Another was Rabbi Isaiah Levy of England, a first cousin of Mrs. Klein, who had been chosen to take Dr. Klein's place. The address was delivered by Rabbi Herbert Goldstein, the founder and spiritual leader of the Institutional Synagogue, which was located across the street from the Ohab Zedek Synagogue, and president for many years of the Union of Orthodox Congregations of America, himself a graduate of my alma mater. My father, assisted by the Ohab Zedek choir sang most of the Sheva Berachot (the seven benedictions) following the Birchot

Erusin (the betrothal blessings), some of them being recited by his pupil and protege, Cantor Samuel Malavsky.

Among the guests in attendance was my colleague Rabbi Israel M. Goldman, who, after ministering to Temple Emanuel of Providence, Rhode Island, for twenty-one years, was called to succeed Rabbi Adolph Coblenz as rabbi of the Chizuk Amuno Congregation of Baltimore. We have remained fast friends until this day and are presently, in addition thereto, neighbors.

Small Reception

Even if my father and father-in-law had been as rich as Croesus, it is doubtful whether they could have invited all those who attended the wedding ceremony to the meal that usually follows the nuptials. Because it was difficult to draw a line and in order not to offend their numerous friends, the wedding dinner was restricted to family and nearest of kin. I was a bit embarrassed by the fact that the members of the board of my congregation, who had come all the way from Trenton, could not be invited.

It was quite late by the time Claire and I were able to retire to our suite in the Astor Hotel and be completely alone for the first time in our lives. I shall skip over this initial phase of our matrimonial career because what transpires between husband and wife is not for publication. Suffice it to say that life with Claire was bliss from the start, and it has remained that way throughout the years.

For various and sundry reasons we were unable to indulge in the luxury of a honeymoon trip. One was that the academic semester began the next day and I had to meet my pupils in Columbia University. Another was that I could not afford to neglect my flock in Trenton. Most important of all, however, was the fact that the marriage of my brother Leo was scheduled for the Wednesday following mine, and that my sister Nettie was to be married on the Saturday night after his wedding.

It is rare for three members of the same family to celebrate their nuptials within one week and not entirely in keeping with Jewish custom. But what else could we do when our father was so pressed for time? There was, therefore, no chance for us newlyweds, myself and Claire, to get away even for a few days. However we made up for this by subsequent trips together, which more than took the place of the honeymoon we missed.

Getting Settled

The part of Trenton in which the handsome, recently constructed synagogue of Congregation Adath Israel was located, and in the vicinity of which we settled, at the outskirts of this capital of the state of New Jersey, was lovely and picturesque. We were fortunate in being able to rent from the treasurer of the congregation. Mr. Siegel, the comfortable one-story brick house that he had just built for his daughter next-door to his own but was never occupied by her. The street was part of a residential neighborhood of private cottages, green lawns, shady trees, and comparatively little traffic. Our only complaint was that we never seemed to get enough heat. But this problem did not present itself until the winter. Also, some of our furniture was late in arriving.

Mrs. Siegel was a lovely motherly lady, whose chief worry was that my young wife was not feeding me sufficiently. However Claire very quickly mastered the culinary arts of cooking and baking, and I can testify to the excellence of her cuisine.

On account of her small frame and her slender figure Claire looked at twenty-one no older than a girl of sixteen. The consequence was that when the new rebbetzin was introduced to one of the officers of the sisterhood, that lady glanced straight over her head and asked "Where?"

XXVI

The Year in Trenton

THE FIRST YEAR is undoubtedly the crucial, or test, period of a marital career. It is during that time that a man and a woman, bound by the ties of wedlock, find out whether they are compatible and fit into each other's lives. They must, of course, learn to adjust if their marriage is to last.

For all that we had in common Claire and I most certainly constituted two distinct and different personalities. She was the more sensitive member of the team and had to wait to be in a mood for carrying out certain chores, while I was more energetic. She was talkative, alert, and always ready to do what had to be done. I was more taciturn, subject, perhaps on account of my study habits, to spells of absent-mindedness. She was interested in personal matters. My chief concern was issues, causes. She liked to read late. I had to go to sleep early in order to be up in time for the morning services. However we both loved music, liked to travel, see new sights, admired works of art, and enjoyed good literature.

It was fortunate that I had secured a position outside of New York. It enabled us to grow together more quickly, to become more dependent on ourselves in solving our problems and settling differences and less tied to the family apron strings. Trenton was only an hour's distance by train from the homes of the parents of both of us, so it was still possible to visit them fairly frequently without too much loss of time. On the other hand, the mere fact of living in another city gave us greater privacy and rendered us relatively immune to the growing difficulties that beset our elders.

That first year of our married life, which Claire and I spent in Trenton, had its compensations. But it was far from being free from anxiety and even a certain amount of physical discomfort. To begin with, Claire became pregnant shortly after our marriage, and while her pregnancy was completely normal, she did not always feel up to par. I was too much preoccupied with writing my dissertation to give her the attention I should have shown her. Furthermore, while preparing sermons for every Sabbath did not come too hard so long as the weekly portions read in the synagogue were taken from the books of Genesis and Exodus, with their rich narrative content, when it became necessary to deliver a message based on the opening sections of Leviticus describing the sacrificial services performed in the tabernacle, the going became rough.

I started working on Sunday morning and by Friday had not yet produced anything that I thought would be of sufficient interest to my congregation. The result was that I had a nervous stomach before preaching. It wore off after a while. Within two years, as my technique improved, the nervousness left me. From then on, since I had made it an unfailing habit to write out what I had to say, I felt completely relaxed whenever I spoke in public.

The chief cause of my restlessness was, of course, the uncertainty about the permanence of my position in Trenton. Commuting twice a week to New York in order to teach at Columbia University, coupled with the possibility of missing the train, was rather exhausting. Most of all, however, what troubled me was the question of whether I would succeed in turning a congregation that had been founded as Conservative back to Orthodoxy.

The Youth

I had been told that it all depended on the feelings of the youth, and I was issued carte blanche to exercise upon the younger generation my powers of persuasion. In my naivete and lack of experience, I took those who had given me this assurance at their word and set out immediately to try my skill.

A meeting was called of all the young people under thirty-five. The response was overwhelming, and when I had finished making my presentation, indicating that Judaism had traditions of its own, which differ from those of Christianity, such as covering the head during prayer, praying in the language that is common to Jews all over the world, and separation of the sexes in the synagogue, over ninety percent of those present were ready and willing to follow my lead.

When the president heard of these results, he declared the vote illegal because the meeting had not been called by him and was, therefore, not official. In order to satisfy the provisions of the constitution another session was arranged, this time under the imprimature of the elected lay head of the congregation. Again I had the majority with me, but not as large as the one previous. I was wondering seriously whether, under the circumstances, I should stay. It would have meant a fight and a possible split of the congregation, which I was anxious at all costs to avoid.

However, what finally decided me to sever my connection with Adath Israel was the fact that on the last day of Passover, at the Yizkor service, a vice-president of the congregation, who was unable to pronounce properly the few English readings with which we interspersed the services, in defiance of the agreement made with me, sat down together with his wife. This proved to me beyond the shadow of a doubt that the pretended clamors of the youth were a pretext used by their elders for introducing changes which in their estimation meant progress, a step up in the social ladder. It was the old, not the young, that really asked for it. This was my first brush with synagogue politics. However it be, I then and there submitted my resignation, to take effect immediately after Shabuot.

Truth to tell, Trenton did not have enough of a Jewish intelligentsia to satisfy me. If I was to remain in the rabbinate, I wanted to live in a city that had a university with a department of Semitics.

No Hard Feelings

I left Trenton without any hard feelings. My salary was paid in full until the end of the year. If only I could have seen my way clear to accept mixed seating, I would have been awarded a ten-year contract. So much confidence did the leaders of the congregation repose in me that they asked me to suggest a successor. I recommended a classmate and colleague whom I had known since my early public-school years, Leon Liebreich, an excellent Bible student. He served them for eighteen years and with utmost satisfaction.

When our oldest son David was born on July 24, a beautiful luncheon was tendered by the congregation in honor of his initiation into the Covenant (Bris) of Abraham. Also, when the congregation celebrated the silver anniversary of its founding, I was invited as the guest speaker.

Our differences were, then, purely ideological. Nothing personal was involved. We had made a number of friends in Trenton. Closest to Claire was a very attractive young woman by the name of Anne Shirken. We kept in touch with her and her family many years after we had moved out of the city.

XXVII

Doctor of Philosophy

AT THE TIME when I tendered my resignation from Adath Israel of Trenton, I had no idea of what my future would be and whither fate would take me. The only sure plans I had for the month following was that since the manuscript of my doctor's dissertation was in sufficient shape for publication, and I had fulfilled my residence requirements at Columbia University, I was in a position to take my predoctoral examination and defend my thesis.

The date of my appearance before the examining committee was set for May 5. It happened to be my twenty-fifth birthday. To my pleasant surprise, the committee was headed by none other than Dr. W. F. Albright, the director of the American School of Oriental Research in Jerusalem, under whom I had studied and with whom I had been so pleasantly associated during my year's sojourn in the Holy City.

Near Perfect Mark

As for the examination itself, it was a delightful experience. I was not a bit nervous. I answered the oral questions directed at me without hesitancy. Dr. Albright later told me that the committee was very favorably impressed and that I scored a near perfect mark.

Equipped with my seminary ordination, with the traditional semichah acquired in Palestine, and with a Ph.D. from Columbia, for which I first received the diploma when three hundred printed copies of my *Highways to Perfection of Abraham Maimonides* were delivered to the library of Columbia University early in 1929, I was prepared to storm any congregational citadel to which I might be sent.

This time the placement committee of my alma mater got into the act. There was a new congregation in Baltimore, so I was informed, that was anxious to secure a spiritual leader. It was somewhat difficult for the seminary to fill its needs because there were two powerful factions in the congregation, one with strong Orthodox leanings, the other more inclined toward the conception of Judaism held by the overwhelming majority of the graduates of the seminary.

For an entire year candidates, sent by both my alma mater and the Rabbi Isaac Elchanan Rabbinical College of New York, had occupied the pulpit of Beth Tfiloh on Saturdays. Yet for one reason or another none of them suited the different elements of which the congregation, as then constituted, was composed. As a last resort I was recommended.

I had the advantage of being endorsed by Rabbi Herbert Goldstein, the president of the Union of Orthodox Congregations of America, of which Beth Tfiloh's first president, Israel Gomborov, was vice-president, as well as by the institution in which I had received my rabbinical training. A further inducement was the fact that I was a son of Yossele Rosenblatt.

At all events, I preached on a Sabbath toward the end of August in Beth Tfiloh's brand-new sanctuary on the corner of Garrison Boulevard and Dalrymple Avenue. The pews had been installed the week before I came. The quality of my performance secured for me an invitation to deliver the sermons and take over whatever parts of the services were usually conducted by the rabbi on the High Holidays.

XXVIII

Rabbi of Beth Tfiloh

ON THE SATURDAY NIGHT between Rosh Hashanah and Yom Kippur, a meeting was held by the board which ended in my election as rabbi of the Beth Tfiloh Congregation. Its charter stated unequivocally that its religious worship was to be in accordance with the Ashkenazic rite and that no changes were to be effected if there was opposition to such a change by a single member. It was clearly understood that the rabbi was the supreme authority in all matters of Jewish law, and that no adverse vote on the part of the laity could override his veto.

All this suited me perfectly. I made no rash promises to the men who had engaged my services as their spiritual leader for an initial period of two years, other than that I would endeavor to abide by the provisions of the constitution and do my utmost to further the best interests of the congregation. They would have to have confidence in my leadership and not expect the impossible, such as attempting to please everybody and be all things to all people.

In order to carry out my obligations to the men and women who looked to me for direction and guidance, it was necessary that I first be sure in my own mind that what I was doing was right. I would be outspoken and fearless in the expression of my views, but never, under any circumstances, would I single out any individual member of my flock for castigation or censure, and certainly not in public. This was my policy from the very beginning, and I have adhered to it until the present.

My declaration of principles met with the unanimous approval of the spokesmen of the congregation, most of them men in their thirties, who attended that meeting. Among them was the aforementioned Israel Gomborov, his successor at the time in the presidency, Harry T. Kellman, and Joseph Allen, in whose gracious home I made my headquarters from the time when I first came to Baltimore until I moved into my own apartment after the fall holiday season. All three of them were lawyers. Included in the group were also successful industrialists and businessmen, all of whom played a prominent role in the affairs of the synagogue.

Made to Order

Beth Tfiloh seemed to have been made just to order for me. It was Orthodox and yet modern, up-to-date. There was a separation between the men's and women's sections of the synagogue, yet the ladies were not compelled to go high up on a balcony but were accommodated on a slightly elevated area in accordance with the seating arrangements of the Jewish Center in New York. The overhanging balustrade used for the overflow had been reduced in length. It was over this issue that a small minority had pulled out prior to my engagement as rabbi of Beth Tfiloh.

However I soon discovered that agreements in theory are not always adhered to in practice. In fact during the first automobile ride on which he took me, one of the members of the congregation, who was apparently a person of considerable influence, informed me that although Beth Tfiloh was supposed to be a democratic organization, in reality its affairs were run by three people, who constituted its "power-structure" as it were. They included himself and two other individuals. "If there is anything you want to have done, rabbi," he said, "tell us and it will be executed."

Not a Politician

What he had in mind was that, since as rabbi I had the last word in matters of Jewish law, I might by the exercise of the rabbinical prerogative of interpretation sanction innovations that would, in effect, put Beth Tfiloh into the Conservative camp. If this was his calculation, he was, of course, due for keen disappointment, as he and those who sided with him were to discover very quickly. I had no intention of being diverted from the course I had adopted, however great the pressure exerted. As I made it crystal clear in my installation address, I was not a politician, who for the sake of expediency might be swayed to compromise. As a rabbi, chosen to bring the word of God to my flock, I was bound to uphold principle regardless of the price.

Unforgettable Installation

By the way, my formal induction into my duties of office as the spiritual leader of Beth Tfiloh was without question the most inspiring, elevating, and glamorous affair in the entire history of the congregation. It was a truly unforgettable event. The installation exercises were held in the main auditorium of the recently completed synagogue. By 4:30 in the afternoon, which was the time when the program was scheduled to begin, the beautiful sanctuary, built in Moorish-Romanesque style with its tall, black marble columns, was literally filled to the rafters.

The elite of Baltimore were there. Everyone who stood for anything was on hand. There was not a congregation of importance that was not represented. Joseph Allen, who was then in his thirties, presided. He was a superb, eloquent, and witty chairman. President Harry T. Kellman delivered greetings. Dr. Moses Hyamson, my teacher of codes, acting on behalf of my alma mater, gave the installation address. Dr. William Rosenau of the Oheb Shalom Temple, the oldest rabbi in Baltimore from the standpoint of tenure, spoke for the rabbinate of the "Jerusalem of America." Cantor Ilmer of Beth Tfiloh and Cantor Malavsky, who was to succeed him when he resigned two years later, participated.

However the star of the occasion, whose presence was undoubtedly responsible for most of the overflow crowd that had come to see and hear, was my father. His singing was not just magnificent. It was divine. Never did the declaration "the disciples of the wise increase peace in the world," contained in the collection of quotations from the Talmud begining with the words *Omar Rabbi Elozor*, sound so sincere and meaningful as when it was sung by him that evening.

The installation itself was followed by a sumptuous banquet held in the gymnasium of the Community Center building. Rabbi Adolph Coblenz of the Chizuk Amuno, my only fellow alumnus at the time in Baltimore, was the principal speaker.

Sermons and Lectures

That first year of my ministry to Beth Tfiloh was a very busy one for me, its first rabbi. For forty-five years I was able to boast, without immodesty, that I was the best rabbi the congregation ever had, because I was the only one during that period of time to be in charge of the direction of its religious affairs, and there was no one else with whom to make comparisons, favorable or otherwise.

To preach on every Sabbath morning was, of course, the first and principal obligation of every rabbi ministering to a modern American Jewish congregation. It was taken for granted, a sine qua non of the functions of members of the rabbinical profession. What was not so commonplace was the stipulation in my case that one sermon, a month, on the Sabbath preceding the New Moon, was to be delivered in Yiddish, the vernacular of the older generation of Beth Tfilohites, most of whom were immigrants from Eastern Europe. When Claire heard of this arrangement and, to make matters worse, that I had agreed to it, she was aghast. "How could you dare to assume such a task when you have never spoken Yiddish in public?" she asked. Besides she was not much enamored of Yiddish as a medium of communication because, like many natives of Western Europe, she looked down upon it as a sort of jargon, a mongrel speech made up of elements derived from a variety of sources.

However I was not either disturbed or perturbed. Even though the version of Yiddish I had heard at home was the Galician, I was able without difficulty to adapt mine to that which was spoken by most of my parishioners, who were of Lithuanian provenance.

In addition, however, to the Sabbath morning sermons, I delivered lectures in popular form, on Jewish philosophical, biblical, and historical themes at the Friday evenings forums that I instituted during the winter months from the end of Sukkot until Passover. I formed classes for the youth on Sundays and for the women on weekday mornings. I taught the Talmud in Yiddish twice a week between the afternoon and evening services, discoursed on the Chapters of the Fathers on Sabbath afternoons during Shalosh S'udoth (the third meal), and Mishnah in English prior to the Saturday afternoon services.

After the lapse of but a few months after my engagement as rabbi of Beth Tfiloh, that is to say, on February 17, 1928, I launched the publication of the *Beth Tfiloh Messenger*, the congregational weekly, of which I remained the editor and chief contributor for several decades. During the initial period it cost the congregation virtually nothing as most of the expenses were covered by advertisements.

XXIX

Teaching Schedule

THERE WERE AT THAT TIME, among the older members of the Beth Tfiloh Congregation, enough with a talmudic background to justify the formation of a Chevra Shass, a group organized for the study of the Talmud and other works of Jewish lore. In addition to myself, the teaching staff included our sexton, Rev. H. B. Zenitz, a former agent of the *Jewish Daily News*. Always immaculately dressed, he was a man of learning who lent much dignity to his office. Spurning the title of shamash, which signifies, literally "servant" or "waiter," he preferred to be called "superintendent." He taught the agadic portions of the Talmud known as *Ein Yaakov*.

Among the lay instructors the oldest was Mr. Samuel Levy, a professional Hebrew teacher who was really an excellent Bible scholar and expert in Hebrew grammar. Until I appeared on the scene he was the last word in Beth Tfiloh in all matters of Jewish law. That must have been the reason why, at the beginning at least, he resented the usurpation of his authority by a young man in his twenties, like myself. When, however, his pupils boycotted him as chastisement for his uncomplimentary remarks about me, he felt put in his place and recanted, and we became close friends. He conducted the class in Mishnah. After his passing it was taken over by Israel Gomborov and occasionally by Joseph Allen.

So far as the afternoon Hebrew School was concerned, the classes of which were initially conducted five days a week, as well as the Sunday School, which was attended mostly by girls, they had been entrusted, simultaneously with my engagement as rabbi of Beth Tfiloh, to Maurice

L. Perman as principal. Though he was himself hardly more than twenty years old when the responsibility of directing the education of the youth of the congregation was thrust upon him, Perman was a first-rate pedagogue, who had a marvelous rapport with children although he was rather uncomfortable with their parents.

Membership Campaign

The maintenance of these and other activities of the congregation demanded a regular and assured source of income. However up to the time when I was elected as Beth Tfiloh's spiritual leader, there were no such things as regular membership dues. This was, therefore, almost the first task to which I and the lay leadership of the congregation had to address ourselves. An appeal I made on Kol Nidre night resulted in the affiliation of one hundred dues paying members, contributing a total of ten thousand dollars.

During the months following, a two-man team consisting of myself and Mr. Nathan Sollod visited some hundred Jewish families residing in the Forest Park neighborhood. This effort brought the number of affiliates up to two hundred. From then on the congregation experienced a steady growth, so that by the middle forties it reached an all time high of nine hundred members. Never during my entire career did I overlook or neglect an opportunity to persuade newcomers in our community to join our ranks.

Notwithstanding my preoccupation with the affairs of my synagogue, its community center and school, I engaged also in sundry outside activities. As I still served on the faculty of the Semitics department of Columbia University I was compelled at least once a week to commute to New York to give my courses in Arabic and Syriac.

Rayner Fellow in Semitics

I was relieved of these exertions by a vacancy created in this field at the Johns Hopkins University through the demise of the head of the Oriental Seminary, Dr. Paul Haupt, and the tragedy that had befallen the Jewish Egyptologist and Arabist Dr. Aaron Ember, a brother of Mrs. Harry T. Kellman, who was burnt to death in his home.

At the suggestion of Dr. William Rosenau, who was instructor in the Bible and its commentaries at this famous seat of learning, and whose attention had been called to my competence in Semitic languages by Samuel J. Keiser, one of the intellectuals of our congregation and one-time student at the Hebrew Union College, I was appointed, beginning with February of the year 1928, Rayner Fellow in Semitics.

I no longer had to dissipate my energies by spending almost an entire day traveling to and from New York in order to teach for a few hours. Resigning from my post in Columbia, to the regret of Dr. Gottheil, I was given its equivalent at the Johns Hopkins University and I have served on its faculty ever since.

Waking Up the Neighborhood

The change, which was a very welcome one indeed, gave me more time to spend with my family. Our quarters during that first year were rather small and cramped. We lived on the first floor apartment of a two-story brick house on the corner of Norfolk Avenue and Garrison Boulevard, just one short block away from the synagogue.

People who felt uncomfortable parking their cars close to schul would leave their vehicles right in front of our dwelling. David, our first-born who was a whimpering three-month-old infant when we came to Baltimore, though he was a very friendly and precocious child, got so accustomed to crying at night as to wake up nearly the entire neighborhood. One time—it was about three in the morning—he screamed so loud that a passing policeman, knocked at our door to inquire what was going on.

When Claire came out, he gave her a sharp reprimand for allowing a baby to suffer and doing nothing to pacify him. That there may have been some reason for our son's howling is not unlikely. Yet he seemed to be cured of his habit when, upon the advice of our pediatrician, we slammed the door when he started and let him cry till he tired of carrying on.

XXX

Period of Apprenticeship

THAT FIRST YEAR of my ministry to Beth Tfiloh might probably be best characterized as a period of apprenticeship. It would have been of great help to me if, prior to my acceptance of the congregation's call, I had been associated with an older colleague, with practical experience in the rabbinate, to whom I could have turned for advice and guidance. I would thereby have avoided many a blunder inevitable for a novice. As it was, I had to feel my way before gaining complete self-assurance.

Thus, for example, the question was posed to me whether the privilege of reciting the Haftarah (the message from the Prophets following the weekly pentateuchal lesson on Saturdays and the festivals) was to be given to laymen or, in order not to discriminate between members qualified to carry out this assignment and those incapable, it be chanted by the sexton. Since it was not a point of law that was involved, but merely one of usage, I left it to the Religious Service Committee to decide what to do about the matter. This was definitely a mistake. It opened the way for controversy, which might not have arisen had I made up my mind right at the start as to what was more desirable. Peace was at last restored when I decided in favor of the first of the two alternatives. It has been the course followed at Beth Tfiloh ever since.

No Plays to Gallery

But if indecision is a trait of inexperienced youth—and I was at the time all of twenty-five years old—there were certain faux pas of which I was even then rarely ever guilty. Never in my remarks from the pulpit did I single out an individual for reprimand or censure, however much he may have been deserving of it. I addressed myself always to the subject, the cause, the idea, not the person. Secondly, I tried to minister to the needs of my parishioners without distinction, to treat them equally regardless of position or station, wealth or educational background. Never did I make a play for the gallery to curry the favor of the influential and powerful and neglect the rest.

It was fortunate for me that as spiritual leader of Beth Tfiloh I was given complete freedom of the pulpit. I never hesitated to express my point of view. Thus, even though its president at this time, Harry T. Kellman, was the president of the Baltimore Zionist district, I preached Religious Zionism. He tolerated it because he respected my right to convictions, and perhaps also because I did not abuse my privilege by tactlessness and indiscretion. Knowing that there is no person without blemish, that all human beings have shortcomings of one kind or another, I endeavored to see the good in everyone, to overlook the weaknesses of the members of my flock for the sake of their virtues. Also, I never underestimated the intelligence of my listeners. That is why I not only made it a practice never to speak unprepared. Writing out my sermons also helped improve my style, enabled me to avoid unnecessary repetition, and also prevented my wandering away from the central theme.

My chief critic was Claire. It was she who kept me from becoming ponderous and pedantic, which is a common tendency among scholars. By her fine sense of language, which Professor Albright later on detected in her, she inspired me to discipline myself in choosing the most appropriate figures of speech and eliminating the superflous and redundant. There were times when she blue-penciled what I had written as lacking in freshness and novelty. I would think about her strictures, which upon reflection I often recognized as justified, start out afresh, and come up with something much more satisfactory and effective than at first.

Scripture as Guidance

In selecting the topics of my sermons, I generally turned for inspiration to the portion of the week or the prescribed pentateuchal or prophetic reading for the holiday. I was averse to using the text merely as a pretext, however. The lesson contained or implied in the text had to have a direct bearing on the problems of the hour. I considered it my business as a preacher to demonstrate the relevance of the utterances of

Scripture, made nearly three thousand years ago, to the troubles that beset mankind in our day and age. Without such a connection the exposition of a biblical text would be a lecture in ancient history of interest to archaeologists, not to people seeking guidance for working out their personal problems in the word of God.

In order to avoid falling into a uniform groove, I used a different approach every annual cycle. One year my key was the questions raised by Bible criticism. Another year it was the talmudic principles suggested in the weekly portion. A third year I would base my sermons on some characteristic interpretation, in historical sequence, of the outstanding Jewish Bible commentators. A fourth year the titles of my discourses were suggested by the names of the pentateuchal readings. In this way I had fresh messages for my congregation every year, notwithstanding the fact that the text on which they were based remained unchanged. During the forty-nine years that I have occupied the pulpit of Beth Tfiloh, no one ever found it necessary to tell me what to preach on and what to avoid.

Getting Along with Others

To get along with others has been my life-long endeavor, and I have always prided myself on the fact that I have been on speaking terms with all elements of the Jewish population of Baltimore, from the extreme right to the extreme left. On the one hand, Orthodox Jewish institutions of learning of Baltimore often turned to me for assistance. Their representatives knew they could count on my material support and moral encouragement. As for those at the other end of the Jewish spectrum, Dr. William Rosenau, the dean of the Reform rabbinate, was ready to recommend me as a candidate for the chair of Jewish philosophy at the Hebrew Union College. If the offer was declined by me, on ideological grounds, it was, nevertheless, a high compliment to me that it had been made at all.

XXXI

Laying the Groundwork

THAT FIRST YEAR was also the time for laying the groundwork for those units of Beth Tfiloh that enabled it to function not only as a place of worship but also as an institution serving as a means for the discharge of many other religious and social obligations of the congregation's membership.

One important innovation was the selection of a uniform prayerbook that would make it possible for all the worshippers in the synagogue to follow the services without difficulty. My choice for use on weekdays and the Sabbath was the best available in the United States at the time, namely the *Standard Prayer Book*, with the translation of the Rev. S. Singer of England, published by Bloch. It had been adopted by the Chizuk Amuno Congregation, whose mode of worship was then identical with that prevailing at Beth Tfiloh. For the High Holidays and the Pilgrimage Festivals I proposed the *Machzor* of Dr. Adler, former chief rabbi of the United Kingdom, gotten out in America by the Hebrew Publishing Co. of New York. I favored it on account of the excellent renderings of several of the liturgical selections into English by such outstanding Jewish poets of Great Britain as Israel Zangwill and Nina Salaman. Later on the *Adler Festival Prayerbook* for the High Holidays was replaced by the one-volume *Machzor* published by Rabbi Morris Silverman of Hartford, Connecticut.

Page Indicator

However, even with the employment of one and the same book it was necessary, in order to make certain that the congregation would keep up with the cantor, to announce the pages at regular intervals. This would have constituted an interruption of the services, which I was determined at all costs to avoid. Besides it would have necessitated the rabbi's bobbing up almost every time a page was turned. To obviate this annoying disturbance of the solemnity of our devotions I devised page indicators that could be operated manually and noiselessly. These were set up in the front of the synagogue, where they were visible to everybody. My invention was improved upon the year following by one of the most resourceful and useful members of our congregation, A. Zabdiel Levy. A graduate civil engineer, he became the official custodian of Beth Tfiloh's physical plant as well as of its cemetery.

He also assisted in the auxiliary services on the High Holidays, often pinch-hit for the sexton in reading the Torah, and regularly chanted the Book of Esther on the morning of Purim. During the last decade of his life he was the president of the Vaad Hakashrut of Baltimore, which, with the help of knowledgeable and interested laymen like him, I had put on a firm footing when the situation in Baltimore had become so chaotic as to turn off young people anxious to observe the Jewish dietary laws.

The indicators perfected by Zab Levy had no sooner been installed than other Orthodox congregations, hearing about them, applied to the inventor for the gadget. There are now hundreds throughout the United States that are making use of it.

Use of Microphone

However, all the efforts to improve the decorum in our synagogue would have been of but little avail if it had not been possible for all the worshippers to hear the prayers sung by the cantor and the words spoken by the rabbi. Since the main sanctuary had a seating capacity of only six hundred and the demand for accommodations on the High Holidays was already then for at least one thousand, it was necessary to add the Community Center auditorium, which connected with the synagogue by means of sliding doors, in order to take care of the overflow. But the low ceiling of the balcony above cut off completely all sounds coming from the front. When people do not hear, they become restless, and no matter how hard he who presides over the services may try to catch their attention and call them to order, he will be unable to control them since they cannot even make out what he is trying to say.

The only solution was the installation of a microphone. In order to find out how this could be done in keeping with Jewish law (with the halachah), I corresponded with the then recognized rabbinical authorities, whose ruling would be acceptable to the most scrupulous. Four of them—all the men to whom I had written—answered my question affirmatively. Our problem was solved, and within a short time many of my colleagues in the English-speaking Orthodox rabbinate, on the basis of the replies I had gotten, followed our example. If the decision was reversed several decades later by some of the very men who had previously given their approval, this was, I suspect, done not on purely halachic grounds. Other considerations must have figured in the change.

The use of the microphone and the interspersal of explanations and additional readings in English, especially on the High Holidays, contributed in no small measure to maintaining order during our religious services.

Machzikei Torah

The First World War had wrought havoc with the great centers of Jewish life in Eastern Europe. Particularly affected were the yeshivot, the academies dedicated to the study of the Talmud and rabbinic lore in general. Most of them were located in the newly constituted republics of Poland and Lithuania. The cultivation by the elite of the Jewish youth in these countries of their spiritual heritage was pursued with zest and vigor. However, for the financial support of these institutions, those interested in their maintenance were compelled to turn to their kinsmen in America, who had been fortunate enough to escape the ravages of war and many of whom had achieved affluence.

Emissaries from such renowned rabbinical schools as those of Myr, Slabodka, Telshe, and Radin were visiting the United States in ever-increasing numbers. They could certainly not afford to overlook a community like that of Baltimore, with its reputation, whether deserved or not, of being the Jerusalem of America. And once they had come, why discriminate against an up-and-coming congregation like Beth Tfiloh?

So even before I had been engaged as Beth Tfiloh's spiritual leader, appeals for funds by representatives of the aforementioned institutions of learning were made almost every Saturday, and it was the people on hand when these fervent pleas were offered who had to bear a burden that should have been shared by many others. A situation of such a nature could not continue indefinitely. The possibility of being compelled to put their hands in their pockets every time they attended synagogue services might have frightened many would-be worshippers away. Besides, it was unfair that the comparatively few should shoulder an obligation that devolved on all.

This is what motivated me, with the help of a number of conscientious and practical lay members of the congregation, to found the Machzikei Torah ("Supporters of Torah") Society. For a good many years I devoted my sermon on Yom Kippur morning, when Jewish worshippers are in the best mood for listening to discourses on the importance of Jewish learning and the need for supporting those who dedicated their lives toward furthering it, to this subject. Cards with the amounts pledged to be turned down were distributed among all seat-holders.

The sums realized, without the mention of names or figures, during the trying years of World War Two totaled as much as sixteen thousand dollars. The members of Beth Tfiloh still contribute at least seven thousand dollars per annum to yeshivot through its Machzikei Torah Society, which has become a model for other congregations in Baltimore as well as other cities of the United States and Canada.

XXXII

Molding a Congregation

ALL IN ALL, that first year of my ministry to Beth Tfiloh was a challenging but also a rewarding one. It was my task as a young rabbi to take a congregation of very heterogeneous composition, consisting of members of religious backgrounds ranging from almost the extreme right to left of center, and weld it together into a closely knitted unit.

If I succeeded to some extent in achieving this goal, it was due to a number of factors. First of all was the fact that I had a definite program in mind. I was determined to build an edifice combining the best features of the old and the new, one that would symbolize the "beauty of Japheth dwelling in the tents of Shem." Secondly, I concerned myself with every facet of the congregation's life. I took part in all activities, religious, cultural, social, and administrative, in most of which I played a leading role. Last but not least, I was fortunate in securing the cooperation of many fine laymen, young as well as older.

Moving Again

Before the year was up, however, Claire and I again had to face the problem of housing. The two-story duplex, in which we had our apartment, changed hands, and the purchaser intended to occupy it himself. That meant that we had to look for new living quarters in the vicinity of the synagogue, and these were then rather scarce in our neighborhood. We finally located one on Springdale Avenue about five minutes walk from Beth Tfiloh; and in order to avoid the necessity of having to move out again at the end of the year we protected ourselves by means of an option for an additional three-year lease.

The transfer had some rather gratifying consequences for us. Residing on the floor above us were the Schillers, who became our lifelong friends. Claire came to be almost as close to Sarah Schiller as to a sister. Having no children of her own, Sarah virtually adopted ours.

The fall season of my second year at Beth Tfiloh opened auspiciously with a Sabbath morning service conducted by my father, preceded by a Friday night forum, in which he rendered some of his favorite liturgical selections, as well as Zemirot (Sabbath melodies sung at the table). It was an unforgettable Oneg Shabbat (Sabbath joy), and a most pleasant way of launching the series of lectures introducing to those who attended the prophets of Israel and other outstanding personalities in Jewish history.

Contract Renewal

Toward the end of the year my contract came up for renewal. My reelection for a further period of three years was almost unanimous. Thereafter the formalities of a vote were dispensed with. As the successor to Harry Kellman put it: "What need is there for a contract? You are our rabbi. If for any reason we can't get along, no agreement will keep us from parting company, whereas so long as we do, a piece of paper confirming the relationship is superfluous." He was right.

As the only Orthodox rabbi at the time who spoke English without an accent, I was very much in demand, particularly for weddings. The fees for such services were then very modest. Just as I left nothing to momentary inspiration, so far as my sermons in the synogogue were concerned, so did I prepare my messages to the brides and grooms under the nuptial canopy.

The time of the year, outside of the fall and spring festival seasons, when there was a respite from weddings, was the three weeks of mourning extending from the 17th of Tamuz to the 9th of Ab. This is, therefore, the period when most rabbis take their summer vacations. In 1928 Claire and I accepted the invitation of Cantor Ilmer to join him and his wife in a motor tour of Canada. We visited Montreal and Toronto and the Thousand Islands. The next year we spent several weeks with Claire's parents in Arverne, a popular resort on the Long Island seashore. It was almost providential that we did, because Claire's father was already then ailing from an illness that had progressed so far that he lasted only a few months.

XXXIII

A Fateful Year

THE YEAR THAT FOLLOWED was a most fateful one not only for us but for the world in general. It was at the end of 1929 that the New York stock-market crashed and fortunes were wiped out not only in New York but in Baltimore and cities throughout America. Our congregation was among the comparatively small number that held firm. The budget was carefully watched and economies were effected wherever possible. It even established a new affiliate, the brotherhood, and acquired land for a cemetery of its own, which was dedicated not long after. Both these projects had my active support.

Before this happened, in November, my father-in-law, Isser Woloch, passed away. In keeping with his instructions, his body was shipped to the Holy Land for burial. Rummaging through his papers, I found clippings from newspapers listing the prizes I had won when I graduated from Townsend Harris Hall, the high school I attended, at the age of sixteen, together with my picture. That was several years before I had had any thought of wooing his daughter. He had apparently already then had his eye of me. His untimely death imposed responsibilities upon me and Claire, which we assumed cheerfully even though no demands were made by the stricken family.

Nineteen-thirty stands out in my mind as the year which brought with it a change in the personnel of our congregation as well as in my status at the Johns Hopkins University. It was in June of that year, when his contract as Beth Tfiloh's first professional cantor expired, that the Rev. Bernard Ilmer relinquished the post he had held. Whether he did so because he had been offered something better or he sensed that his services were no longer wanted I do not know. The fact is that, as the congregation grew, there were among its members lovers of chazanuth like the late Joseph Leaderman, who would travel many miles to hear a good cantor.

These Beth Tfilohites were anxious to engage an interpreter of the prayers of the synagogue of outstanding ability and renown. They recognized one in Cantor Samuel Malavsky, the pupil and protege of my father, whom they remembered from his participation in the program on the evening of my installation.

In order to enable the congregation to pay Mr. Malavsky an adequate salary, a number of interested men of means volunteered to increase their dues to make up the difference between what was allocated in the budget and the amount that was required.

So far as his performance at the amud (prayer desk) was concerned, Cantor Malavsky completely fulfilled the expectations of those responsible for engaging his services. He was really able, when he was in the mood, to move the congregation by his rendition of the prayers. He was an expert in improvisation and used his voice, even though it was not cultured, his coloratura and falsetto, quite effectively.

Nonconformist

Unfortunately he was temperamental, an inveterate noncomformist. He refused to be bound by rules and was a cynic besides. He never stayed with any congregation more than a few years because, as he himself expressed it, he conceived a dislike for any president he might have in the future. Each one of his six children—they were as handsome as he was and he adored them—was born in a different state of the union. The consequence of all this was that he was with Beth Tfiloh only a year and a half when we had to let him go.

For me personally it was good that he left, because his influence was far from wholesome. He did his utmost to make me discontented with my lot and follow his example of looking for greener fields elsewhere instead of staying put and establishing those ties which only a long tenure makes possible.

W. F. Albright

About the same time that Beth Tfiloh engaged its new cantor, the Johns Hopkins University succeeded in filling the vacancy created in its

Oriental Seminary by the death in 1926 of Professor Paul Haupt. The man chosen as the head of the department, which is now known as that of Near Eastern Studies, was one of the most illustrious alumni of Baltimore's famous seat of higher learning and scientific research, the then thirty-nine-year-old director of the American School of Archaeology in Jerusalem, W. F. Albright.

For me the appointment to the faculty, on which I already served, of this most outstanding biblical scholar and archaeologist of our age, who was also a wonderful human being and one of the best friends Israel and the Jewish people in general have had, was a bit of providential good luck.

My close association with him, which lasted more than four decades, was a joy as well as an inspiration. It was he who encouraged me, busy clergyman that I was, with a large congregation to take care of, to devote whatever time I could steal from my many commitments, to further study and research in my chosen fields of scholarship and to publish my findings. He also contributed to my academic advancement.

Delighted with the favorable reception that had been accorded my doctoral dissertation, which specialists in medieval Jewish philosophy like Professor Wolfson of Harvard hailed as a mature work of scholarship, he was glad to have me as one of his associates.

Scholarly Publications

The other was Professor Frank R. Blake, then still principal of the Baltimore City College and an expert in the grammars of fifty-two languages. Professor Albright welcomed the appearance in 1935 of my little book entitled *The Interpretation of the Bible in the Mishnah*, which threw light on the fine understanding of the subtleties of the language of the Hebrew Scriptures displayed by the authors of this oldest collection of Jewish traditions. He accepted my conclusions to such a point that he quoted them in his own masterpiece, *From the Stone Age to Christianity*.

He was also very pleased to learn that the American Council of Learned Societies had awarded me a grant, which enabled me to secure from the Leningrad library the photostat of a manuscript of a part of Abraham Maimonides' *Highways to Perfection*. By clearing up certain difficulties in the Bodleian manuscript, which was in my possession, it became possible for me in 1938 to publish in a book of 441 pages four-fifths of the Judeo-Arabic text of the philosophical work of the son of Moses Maimonides, which had been the subject of the thesis that had earned me my Ph.D.

By the way, what the curators of the Russian library demanded in payment for the preparation of the photostat was not a draft or money order for the cost, but a number of American manuals on physics and chemistry. The data concerning the titles and the names of the publishers of these books were so accurate that within less than a month they were assembled and shipped, and half a year later I had my photostat.

Professor Albright had no sooner taken charge of his position than he promoted me from Rayner fellow in Semitics to the rank of lecturer in Jewish literature. In addition to Jewish history and other Judaica, such as Mishnah and medieval Hebrew Bible commentaries, I was given the assignment of teaching the elements of the Arabic and Syriac languages and their literatures.

Lectureship in Jewish Literature

However, the university, which paid even him a ridiculously small salary, had no funds whatever for the modest stipend that I was to receive. The only means of solving the problem was to raise the amount required among interested persons in the form of annual subscriptions. Jewish philanthropists of the time, like the late Jacob Blaustein, Aaron Straus, Jacob Epstein, and L. Manuel Hendler, were approached. They responded cheerfully. The lectureship became a reality, and my appointment was assured.

The experience had some gratifying by-products. It was heartwarming for me to come into personal contact with prominent Baltimore Jews outside of my own congregation and to secure their support in raising the prestige of Jewish culture and learning in the general academic world.

XXXIV

Time Marches On

ON FEBRUARY 12, 1931, Lincoln's Birthday, our second son was born. We called him Judah Isser—Judah after my maternal grandfather, Isser after Claire's father, who had passed away fifteen months previously. David, our first born, who was named after his mother's paternal grandfather, was then three and a half years old. After he had overcome his initial indisposition, he turned out to be the easiest child to discipline. He was gentle, courteous, and kind. His younger brother, Judah, was in many respects as different from him as he could possibly be. He was volatile, fiery, quick-tempered, defiant, at times difficult to handle, yet very lovable. Nevertheless the two boys had this in common. They were both bright, intelligent, quick in absorbing knowledge, and in addition thereto honest and sincere. They brought us much joy, were well liked by our parishioners, and made us very proud by their accomplishments.

In the meantime, the economic situation in our country as well as in the world was steadily deteriorating, portents of troubled times ahead. People lost their fortunes. Unemployment increased. Salaries were cut. Some congregations had become completely insolvent. Notwithstanding his world renown, my father, too, was affected. After having served as cantor of the Anshei Sfard of Borough Park for three years, he was compelled to go back to his first connection, Ohab Zedek, which, having moved to the West Side, was then still able to pay wages to its officials.

Kotlowitz Succeeds Malavsky

As for Beth Tfiloh, it could no longer afford a cantor as expensive as Samuel Malavsky and shoulder, besides, the cost of the choir conducted by Samuel Bugatch, the resourceful scion of a well-known Jewish musical family of Baltimore. The board would not have dismissed Malavsky. However, he resigned of his own accord. The chief reason for his termination of his services was that he was averse to leading in congregational singing at the Friday-night forums and on other occasions. So the congregation was again faced with the problem of looking for a man who would not only chant the prayers on Sabbaths and holidays but be in charge of the musical program of the school as well.

Among those recommended was the then thirty-seven-year-old Cantor Max Kotlowitz. A native of Lomza, Poland he had begun his singing career as a member of the Jewish Legion, which had seen service with General Allenby in Palestine towards the end of World War One. He had officiated in Long Branch and Patterson, New Jersey, as well as White Plains, New York. My father, who knew him, spoke highly of his ability as an impresario, composer, and singer of Jewish folk songs and a competent musician with an adequate voice. His description of Max (Mendele) Kotlowitz, as we found out later, turned out to have been very accurate. Whatever Kotlowitz may have been lacking, when compared to Malavsky, in cantorial virtuosity, he more than made up for by other qualities, and he served Beth Tfiloh for twenty-nine years.

His greatest contribution was probably the emphasis he put on congregational participation in chanting the prayers of the synagogue. Beth Tfiloh came to be known as a singing congregation, thanks to the melodies introduced by its cantor. When the worshippers are not just listeners to the solos of the star performer but are given an opportunity to take an active part in the singing, their fervor increases. They derive personal satisfaction from the role they play and are less prone to talk during services.

Purim Plays

A second important service rendered by Cantor Kotlowitz were the Purim plays he wrote, rehearsed and produced in the course of several years in succession. By involving many members of the brotherhood and sisterhood, with talent for acting or singing, he not only assured capacity audiences, which brought the congregation a considerable income during the lean years of the depression. He also generated a spirit of comradery among all the constituents of Beth Tfiloh, which served as an inducement to outsiders to join the fold.

I recognized the value of what he had to offer, and we worked together harmoniously. I was very careful not to trespass on his territory. Outside of chanting the Neilah service on the Day of Atonement, which had long been the prerogative of the rabbi, and of which he was glad to be relieved since he was by that time of the fast day quite exhausted, I rarely ever, during the twenty-nine years of our association, took his place at the amud.

Last but not least, Max Kotlowitz was a sincere and ardent Zionist. By means of his persuasive powers he increased to unprecedented heights the rate of giving to the Jewish National Fund in the city of Baltimore, the income of which had theretofore been derived from pennies and dimes thrown into the JNF collection boxes.

Acquiring a Home

Toward the end of the summer of 1932, when Max Kotlowitz was engaged by Beth Tfiloh as its cantor, the lease we had on our apartment on Springdale Avenue expired, and we again had to cast about for living quarters. Although the time did not seem propitious and the future was uncertain, and despite the fact that rabbis were, on the whole, more on the move than other members of the "wandering people," we decided, in order not to be in such a position for a considerable while, to invest in a permanent abode.

The real estate market was then at its lowest ebb. Homes were available in Forest Park for very little. On the same street as ours but a block closer to the synagogue, a twenty-year-old English-style cottage, two stories high, complete with cellar and attic, constructed of brick and stucco, was offered for sale by the heirs of the owners, who had just died. We acquired it for a price that now, in retrospect, would appear ridiculously low. Yet at the time what we had to pay for it was quite an undertaking. It remained our home for thirty-four years.

Our new residence was gracious and spacious. It was roomy enough to house my constantly growing library. It also made it possible for small weddings to be performed for couples—and there were a good many of them—who could not afford the expense of having their nuptials solemnized in hotels or halls. Very few of the marriages thus begun ended in divorce.

Shortly after we had moved into our home, a member of our sisterhood brought us a cake she had baked for us as a housewarming gift. We were deeply touched by her thoughtfulness but simply could not think of her name so to express our appreciation. Just then our David showed up. It was his habit, whenever he met a stranger, to introduce himself and then ask the other party for his or her name. He did it in this instance also. Thus we got the information we needed and were spared embarrassment.

XXXV

Father's Death

IT WAS FORTUNATE that we had purchased our home when we did, because shortly thereafter my father's material plight had become so acute that I felt I had to do something substantial to relieve him of his pressing burdens. Notwithstanding a voluntary cut in my salary, I had managed to put aside a few thousand dollars for a rainy day.

I offered him these, my last savings, to tide him over the emergency. But it was like pouring sand into a sack full of holes. Actually I had no illusions about ever recovering what seemed to me then a considerable sum of money. But I felt no qualms about doing what I had done, because, if I hadn't helped my conscience would never have given me rest.

That summer was the last for my father to make a public appearance in Baltimore. It was in the form of a musical recital at the Lyric. He also sang for the inmates of Levindale, Baltimore's Jewish home for the aged, on the lawn of that institution. An audience of over one thousand came to listen to him, and the applause was deafening.

In spite of the depression my father was kept busy by engagements that took him all over the United States, until the end of March 1933. However the debt he had incurred by his ill-fated newspaper venture, far exceeded his diminished earnings.

The Last Journey

So, in the hope of being able to recoup some of his losses, he allowed himself to be persuaded to accept the rather uncertain offer of a group of entrepreneurs to tour Palestine, Rumania, and Czechoslovakia. Hitler had just come to power and thousands of well-to-do German Jews, in order to elude him, had settled in the Jewish homeland, bringing about thereby a brief era of prosperity.

The people who had made the arrangements for my father's performances in the synagogues on the Sabbaths and holidays, and the concerts to be given by him on weekdays, expected to reimburse themselves for the expenses of the journey for him and my mother and Henry out of the proceeds from these functions. They also promised him compensation for his services.

Truth to tell, my father had looked forward with eager anticipation to the trip. It had been his lifelong wish to visit the Holy Land and eventually make it his home. There was nothing anymore, except his children, to whom he was very much attached, to keep him in America. So he went quite willingly to the age-old land of Jewish hopes and dreams, which was then still in the initial stages of rejuvenation and rebirth.

I had a foreboding when I went to see him off on the *Vulcania*, worn out as he was by care and worry, that I might never see him again. The crush on the ship, which was bound for Palestine, was, on account of the many relatives and friends that had gathered on deck to bid the travelers farewell, such that my little David, whom I had taken along, was almost smothered.

The ten weeks spent by my father in Eretz Yisroel (the Land of Israel) resembled, as I remarked in my account of his life *Yossele Rosenblatt*, the triumphal march of a victorious general. He was literally carried on the shoulders of countless admirers, who idolized him as no other cantor before him had been.

Not even his distinguished colleague, Zavel Kwartin, who was then already living in Palestine, had gotten so enthusiastic a reception. Unfortunately, father's triumph was short-lived. As my heart had told me, he never came back home to America. On June 19, the day after the assassination of the young Zionist Labor leader Chaim Arlosoroff, he died in the Jerusalem he loved. He had sung about it so movingly that the statement made by Judah Halevi, the Hebrew poet of medieval Spain, about himself could very well have been applied to him. He was, indeed, "the harp of its songs."

My father's premature death—he was only fifty-one years old at the time of his demise—was a stunning blow, not only to Jews everywhere but to the musical world in general.

The phonograph, which had been invented just as he began his career as a singer of the synagogue, had brought his mellifluous voice, and the selections from the liturgy for which he had composed the music, to the attention of music-lovers and musicians of all races and creeds. However, no one was as deeply affected by his sudden departure from the world as his own family, especially his wife.

Mother, who survived him by thirty-three years—as long a period of time as the duration of her marriage to him—never fully recovered from the shock. How could she, after all the honors and glory that she had shared with him and the great and the famous, with whom she had been brought into contact, by virtue of her relationship to him? It was a struggle for mother, who had, on account of my father's financial difficulties shortly before his death, been left completely unprovided for, and for the five unmarried children, who lived with her, to just barely get along.

Responsibility

Like others under similar circumstances, I assumed a large share of the responsibility for her maintenance and that of my brothers and sisters until they were able to be on their own. What made it particularly difficult was the fact that my salary had been drastically reduced when, on the very day on which my parents left for Palestine, President Roosevelt closed all the banks in our country. Even at that I was better off than many of my colleagues, who were compelled to give up posts they had held for years because the congregations they served were no longer in a position to live up to their contracts with them.

Although the take-home pay I received was less than it had been theretofore, it was at least assured. Beth Tfiloh has never defaulted.

Furthermore the dollar went much further then than it does today. So we were able to make out. How we and others survived the crisis is still a mystery to me.

Those were indeed times to try men's souls, much worse than what is being experienced now. Only we were too close to what was happening to be aware of the seriousness of the situation. It was against such a background that I planned my second trip to Palestine.

XXXVI

To Visit Father's Grave

IN THE YEAR 1933 commercial aviation was not yet even in its infancy. It was only six years earlier that Charles Lindberg had made his historic solo flight across the Atlantic in his *Spirit of St. Louis*, and more than two decades were to roll by before regular transportation by air from the United States to Israel was inaugurated.

The only way by which a resident of America could get to Palestine was by boat and rail. That is why it was utterly impossible for me to be present at my father's funeral or his interment in the Mount of Olives cemetery on the outskirts of Jerusalem. So I observed the traditional seven days of mourning at home and, when the week was up, went to New York to attend the memorial tribute tendered by the Cantors' Association of America in Carnegie Hall.

Grief

That great temple of music was filled to overflowing by a public steeped in grief. Hundreds wept when the El Mole Rachamim was intoned over the passing of the sweet singer in Israel, whose voice was stilled forever. I determined there and then that, if distance had prevented me from being on hand when my father's remains were laid to rest, I would make it my business to at least participate in the dedication of the monument erected over his grave around the time of the anniversary (Yahrzeit) of his death. But how? Where could I pick up, at a time of universal depression, the amount of money required for such a journey?

I therefore conceived the plan of organizing a pilgrimage to the Holy Land. Despite the fact that fortunes had been lost in the crash of 1929 and the years immediately following there were still some people of means left who had not been too seriously affected.

There were widowers and widows able to muster what a trip to Palestine via Italy and Egypt would cost. They would never have made the trip were it not for the opportunity of traveling with a man who, besides being their spiritual leader, could also tell them something about the history and background of the places they would visit.

So not long after the announcements of the tour had appeared in the *Beth Tfiloh Bulletin* and the *Jewish Times* of Baltimore, fifteen would-be pilgrims, among them retired merchants, schoolteachers and officers of Hadassah had signed up and paid. It was a novel idea. I was a real pioneer in the field. To the best of my knowledge, it had not been tried before by any rabbi, certainly not in Baltimore. However, what I lacked in experience, at least so far as handling people was concerned, catering to their needs and meeting various contingencies, I made up for in enthusiasm and optimism. Claire's contribution to the success of our venture was her charm and her concern for the personal well-being and comfort of each of our companions.

First Pilgrimage to the Holy Land

Before we set sail on June 23 on the prize ship of the Italian Line, the *Rex*, a memorial concert was held in honor of my father at Beth Tfiloh. The time of the function was the night of May 3, which coincided with Lag b'Omer, the break in the period of mourning between Passover and the Feast of Weeks. It was a most inspiring evening. The audience was particularly moved by the playing of a recording by my father of his Elokay Neshomoh, which seemed most appropriate for the occasion on account of the statements in it that "as long as my soul is within me I thank Thee, Lord of all souls" and "Thou art destined to taken my soul from me and also to restore it to me." The sound of his voice sounded so strong and robust as to produce the feeling that he had really not died, but that "Joseph was still alive."

Finally, after having made arrangements for substitutes to occupy my pulpit during the six weeks of my absence, and putting our two little boys in charge of Claire's mother, we were able to leave.

The voyage across the Atlantic into the Mediterranean via the Straits of Gibraltar was a sheer delight. Our fellow travelers were most congenial and intelligent people. We got along very well and remained lifelong friends.

Among the members of our party was a dear elderly lady by the name of Augusta Strauss. Raised in an assimilated German Jewish home, she had married a man who adhered strictly to the Orthodox Jewish way of life. She adjusted completely to her husband's practices, which she continued after his death. She was the only person in our group, outside of myself, who fasted the entire twenty-four hours of the Ninth of Ab (Tish'ah b'Av), not putting a morsel of food into her mouth before three stars appeared in the sky. Out of deference to her, Claire refrained scrupulously from smoking in her presence. Despite the fact that she was a rabbi's wife, Claire did not think it was reprehensible for her or other women to smoke, any more than she regarded taking part in a sociable game of bridge or canasta as unbecoming to a rebbetzin. One evening, when we returned to our cabin, we found, stuck under Claire's pillow, a pack of cigarettes bearing the legend "To Claire Rosenblatt with the compliments of Gussie Strauss."

One week after our departure from New York our ship anchored in Naples, and after a night's stopover we continued our journey by another steamer to Alexandria, the principal seaport of Egypt, founded twenty-three centuries ago by Alexander the Great. Thence we proceeded by train to Cairo, the fascinating capital of this ancient land, which has, since Israel became an independent Jewish state, been out of bounds for Jews. There were then about seventy thousand adherents of Judaism living in Egypt, sixty-four percent of them resided in Cairo and thirty-two percent in Alexandria. A good many were quite prosperous and played a prominent role in commerce, industry, and the professions. Their chief rabbi, Nahoum Effendi, who died in his late eighties, was a respected member of the Royal Academy of Egypt. The owner of the largest department store, where we shopped, was a man by the name of Cohen.

Among the sights we were taken to see were several of the most famous mosques, including that which housed the El-Azhar University, the principal Moslem seat of learning in the world. It reminded us very much of the East European yeshivot of two generations ago except that the students, instead of sitting on benches, squatted on the floor. It was a privilege also to visit the Egyptian museum with its rich treasures of the Egypt of the Pharaohs, notably the jewelry, clothing and art objects found in the tomb of King Tut (Tut-ankh-amen). Most interesting of all were the Sphinx and what were reputed as among the Seven Wonders of the World, the pyramids, those huge mausolea that the ancient rulers of the empire of the Nile had built for themselves with the sweat and toil and at the cost of the lives of thousands of slaves.

XXXVII

Israel in 1934

AN OVERNIGHT RIDE by rail from Cairo took us to Tel Aviv. As we were approaching with bated breath what is now again called the Land of Israel, we heard over the radio the sad news that the Hebrew poet laureate and modern Yehuda Halevi, Chaim Nachman Bialik, had just died. It put a damper on an otherwise unforgettable experience, that of Jews seeing the homeland of their people for the first time.

Tel Aviv, the first houses of which were constructed in the year 1911 on the sand dunes north of Jaffa, was not yet as built up as it is today. The stucco on the older dwellings was still fresh. The cottages were surrounded by lush gardens. The streets were clean and the beaches unpolluted. The neatness and modernization of the shops on such main thoroughfares, as Allenby Street, were evidence of the mark made by the immigration of Jews from Germany with their sense of order and the aesthetic. However, the luxury hotels, which the number-one metropolis of Israel boasts today were not yet in existence. We therefore had to be content with the accomodations offered by the modest two-story hostelry in which we were put up. Considering the fact that Palestine was at that time far from being a haven for tourists, the place was not too bad. However in attempting to decide how to assign the rooms at our disposal, I learned my first lesson as a group leader. That was never to take for granted the obvious. I thought it was the logical thing to have the older folks quartered on the first floor, so that they would be spared the trouble of climbing steps, and send the younger members of our group upstairs. It turned out, however, that their preferences were the direct opposite. So I threw up my hands and let them make their own selection, and everybody was happy.

Outside of this and a few other minor discomforts, this first pilgrimage to the Holy Land which I conducted also had a number of pleasant surprises in store for me. I knew that during the last several weeks of his sojourn in the Land of Israel prior to his unexpected death, my father was rehearsing for a talkie entitled *The Dream of My People*. It pictured him singing on a skiff on the Jordan and in front of the Wailing (now Western) Wall in Jerusalem. Though uncompleted, the film was shown in a number of movie houses in the United States. However, I had never seen it because during the year of mourning following my father's demise I did not go to any theater or listen to music. I wondered, therefore, whether I would ever have a chance to enjoy this last sample of my father's art as a singer. To my good fortune, an outdoor drive-in cinema was located right next-door to our hotel. That same evening *The Dream of My People*, featuring my father looking so alive and singing his famous melodies, was presented on the screen. I was thus able to hear and see perfectly, sitting on the balcony in the back of my hotel room. It seemed, indeed, as though all this had been arranged specially for me.

Jerusalem

After a four-day stay in Tel Aviv, which had grown considerably since I saw it in the spring of 1926, and excursions to the surrounding settlements, we proceeded to Jerusalem. There had been but little change in the general outward appearance of the Holy City in the eight years of my absence. For this credit must be given to the British, whatever fault may be found with their administration of their mandate over Palestine. It was they who saw to it that the traditional style of architecture was preserved. The ancient capital of the Land of Israel was, however, embellished by the addition of a goodly number of imposing public edifices outside of the walls surrounding the Old City.

There was, first of all, on King George Street, the massive King David Hotel, built by them for the accommodation of diplomats, government officials, dignitaries, and prominent visitors. Next to it was the beautiful new YMCA with its tall spires jutting into the sky. Across the street the Jewish Agency had its compound of buildings, constructed of smooth brown sandstone. Nearby was the new synagogue of the Jeshurun congregation, with which I had worshipped during my tenure of the Hazard fellowship at the American School of Oriental

Research. It was constructed in the form of an amphitheater with long narrow windows, just wide enough to admit the light of the brilliant Jerusalem sun without being exposed to its heat.

On top of Mt. Scopus, not too far from Government House, the home of the British high commissioner, rose the sumptuous new Hadassah Hospital, the library of the Hebrew University, the stadium overlooking the Dead Sea, and other units of the university complex. The Yeshivah of Hebron, which I had seen at its old location in the city in which the tomb of the Hebrew patriarchs is located, had been moved to Jerusalem after the disturbances of 1929. It was in the course of these disorders that sixty-four of its teachers and students had been murdered by the Arab mob, inflamed by the mufti, Haj Amin al-Husseini, and permitted to riot at will while the British constabulary was looking away. The yeshivah of Rabbi Kook was still housed in its former headquarters, which had neither running water nor modern plumbing. We visited all these places and other sites of interest, including the Wailing Wall and the narrow lanes and bazaars of the Old City. I had the opportunity to dedicate the monument over the grave of my father on the Mount of Olives. It consisted of a four-foot-high sandstone structure with a beautiful inscription on the slab of stone that covered its top. However, I was disappointed in not finding in town the revered spiritual head of the Ashkenazic community of the Land of Israel, Rabbi Abraham Isaac Kook, in whose school I had studied and who had conferred upon me, eight years earlier, the traditional semichah. I was told that he was away, recuperating from an illness from which he had been ailing of late.

Encounter in Haifa

The Sabbath spent in Jerusalem by our group was a spiritual delight. During the week following, our itinerary took us to Tiberias, Safed, Nazareth, the colonies in the then already lush Valley of Esdrelon, and finally, via Acre, to Haifa. The Technion was still housed in its first headquarters in Hadar Hacarmel, the middle level of what was then Palestine's principal seaport, which the British were in the process of enlarging, as well as the chief industrial city of the old-new land. The campus of Israel's equivalent of America's MIT on top of Mt. Carmel had not yet been conceived of, and the plush Dan-Carmel Hotel was still a distant dream. We were put up in a modest pension overlooking the Bay of Haifa and were quite content. I had learned that the hotel adjacent to ours had a little synagogue at which services were held regularly, and I decided to join the worshippers in their devotions on the morning after our arrival. Claire tried to dissuade me. "You are on vacation, Sam. Your prayers will be just as acceptable if you recite them in privacy and not cut down on your much-needed sleep by getting up so early." However I persisted, and my zeal was rewarded. For whom should I meet at the morning services but Rabbi Kook himself?

He recognized me at once, and was as happy to see me as I was to see him. He extended to me an invitation to come with Claire to visit him in his apartment that afternoon, and we spent several very pleasant hours with him and Mrs. Kook. The conversation, as I recall, revolved for the most part about my father, to whom the rabbi had become very much attached during my parents' all-too-brief sojourn in the Holy Land. He also asked me about my activities in the rabbinate, at the Johns Hopkins University, and in the Mizrachi movement, of the Baltimore chapter of which I had just then been elected president. My encounter with this giant of the spirit, this finest combination of Jewish scholarship and love of Israel that the Jewish nation in the making was fortunate enough to have among its chief architects, during the years prior to its formal birth, was truly exhilarating. It left me with a deep feeling of satisfaction. My pilgrimage to the Land of Israel had not been in vain, if for no other reason than that of having had the privilege of meeting him at such close range. It was also to be the last time, for a year later, while I was attending the 19th Zionist Congress in Lucerne, Switzerland, word came to the delegates that this universally beloved religious leader, Israel's first chief rabbi, had been removed to the world of eternity.

XXXVIII

Italy

FROM HAIFA the S.S. *Martha Washington* bore us to Brindisi, at the southern tip of Italy. From that town, which had boasted in the ninth and tenth centuries a flourishing Jewish community, we were to travel by express to Rome, the capital of Italy. However, since our ship arrived behind schedule, we were compelled to take a local, with a changeover at Foggia. There is where my knowledge of Italian proved to be very useful. We had exactly fifteen minutes to transfer forty-two pieces of luggage from one train to the other. Had I not been able to make myself understood to the porters, who knew not a word of English, this would never have been accomplished, and we would have been compelled to spend an entire day in idleness in this unprepossessing, drab Italian hamlet.

Rome "the eternal" was as fascinating as it was exciting. It had so much to offer of the old and the new, the ancient, the medieval, and the modern, that the eye was simply not sated with seeing nor the ear with hearing. Of greatest interest to our party as Jews were the magnificent synagogue, erected at the beginning of the present century, and the Arch of Titus, built nineteen hundred years ago to commemorate that second Flavian emperor's conquest of Judea and the destruction by his army of the Second Temple of Jerusalem. On one of the inside walls of this monument were carved on stone the figures of Jewish captives carrying the seven-branched candelabrum, the only replica of that famous utensil of the revered shrine to have been preserved for posterity.

Everything had gone smoothly during the first five weeks of our pilgrimage. We were met at every station by agents of our travel agency, transported to our hotels, and accompanied on the sightseeing trips. We stayed together as a group. On the last day of our stay in Rome, however, just as we were boarding the train that was to take us to Naples to meet the *Conte di Savoia*, which was to leave for New York on the day following, it was noticed that one member of our party was not on hand. Seventy-year-old Mr. Ford, the first person to sign up for the tour, the man who had taken hold of my sleeve and vowed never to let go of me, had stopped for a drink in the restaurant of the railroad station but did not show up again. Though we had him paged and looked for him frantically everywhere, we were unable to locate him. As the train was about to pull out, I told Claire to go on ahead with the rest of the party while I would remain behind in the hope of finding Mr. Ford.

Missing Ward

That night I did not sleep a wink. However, all my efforts, my checking with the stationmaster and my notification of the chief of police and the American embassy, were fruitless. No one was able to tell me anything about the possible whereabouts of my missing ward. Finally, all unnerved and in order not to miss my ship and disappoint all the people who had booked me for weddings and other engagements at home, I decided to take a chance by hopping the last train that would get me to Naples in time for the ship's departure, hoping against hope that somehow or other Mr. Ford would make an appearance. Fortunately my prayers were answered. I got off at the first of the two railroad stations in Naples, and there was Claire waving to me that Mr. Ford had been found.

What had happened was that, instead of ascending the train bound southward for Naples, he entered the one headed north for Milan. When the conductor realized that a mistake had been made, he sent Mr. Ford back to Rome and from there to Naples. Arriving in Naples common sense told our man to go to the Hotel Londra, where we had lodged when we first came to Italy. There he was directed to the Toledo, which had been opened up specially to accommodate our group after Claire had refused to accept no for an answer from the managers of the Londra, which, she learned, was all filled. For some unaccountable reason the arrangements had become fouled up. For the first time during our entire trip no one was awaiting our party. It was with a sigh of relief that I ascended the gangplank of the *Conte di Savoia*, after having made sure that all our luggage had been put on board, and there wasn't even an hour left in which to do it. Just then a call came from the American ambassador's office in Rome inquiring whether Mr. Ford had been located. I was so deeply touched by this solicitude on the part of the representative in Italy of our government that all I could do was to exclaim, "God bless America."

More Worries

But if anyone were to think that my worries were thereby at an end, he would be greatly mistaken. On the last night of a very pleasant voyage homeward, one of the stewards knocked at my cabin door to inform me that one of our people, a prince of a man if there ever was one, had had a heart attack. Since the ship's doctor spoke only Italian, there was need for someone to serve as an interpreter and translate his instructions to the patient into English. I seemed to be the only person on board ship who could do it. We managed to make Mr. Friedlander, who had joined our tour in defiance of the advice of most of the physicians he had consulted, and spent the entire two weeks of our sojourn in Israel in bed, as comfortable as we could. In the morning, when the ship was ready to dock, we brought him up on a wheelchair so that he could be taken at once to a hospital. It was with fear and trepidation that I watched the faces of Mr. Friedlander's daughters when they caught sight of their father in this condition. However, they accepted what had happened in the best of spirits. After several weeks of recuperation in a New York sanitarium, Mr. Friedlander was able to return home. He lived for another seven years, attaining an age of close to eighty.

XXXIX

The 19th Zionist Congress

AFTER THESE TWO near disasters in my first venture as the conductor of a tour of the Holy Land, I should have learned my lesson and not attempted anymore to "go where angels fear to tread." However, I was incurable when it came to undertaking tasks from which the cause of Zion was likely to benefit. So I tried to do again in the summer of 1935 what had been so successful in 1934. This time, however, I was unable to secure the desirable accommodations in the ships that were to be used. I therefore contented myself as a consolation with being sent as a delegate of the American Mizrachi to the 19th Zionist Congress, which was to convene in August of that year in my favorite Swiss city of Lucerne.

It was a glorious experience. It gave me an opportunity to see in action leading figures in the world Zionist movement. I had a chance to listen to such towering personalities as Dr. Chaim Weizmann, who had been chiefly responsible for the issuance of the historic Balfour Declaration and was destined to become the first president of the State of Israel when it came into being. I also heard the fiery Menachem Mendel Ussishkin, the mighty oak of the Jewish National Fund. I furthermore met at very intimate gatherings the leaders of Religious Zionism in the United States, Europe, and the Land of Israel. I was afforded a glimpse into the political maneuverings behind the curtain of the various branches of the Zionist family. I learned that even in the country which had been the cradle of the Jewish religion, religion could not flourish automatically. It had to fight for its existence.

To make certain, for example, that the Sabbath and the dietary laws would be observed, at least in the national institutions, those who were deeply concerned about this matter had to be organized so that their voices would be heard and their demands met. This was the raison d'etre of Mizrachi. Thanks to the sizable number of its affiliates at the time in Germany, England, Poland, and Czechoslovakia, this party then controlled one-seventh of the votes in the Zionist Congress and wielded a most wholesome influence in molding the distinctively Jewish character of the Jewish national home and assuring the status in it of the Jewish religion.

Embarrassments

However, my attendance of the sessions of this Congress, the decisions of which were crucial in promoting the success and furthering the progress of the Zionist movement, was not without its embarrassments. Thus, for instance, when I learned that I was among those fortunate enough to be elected as an official emissary to this then highest parliament of the Jewish people, I inquired of someone, who I assumed was familiar with them, about the practices at the Zionist congresses. He informed me that etiquette required the members to appear in full dress on the opening night. This was the custom inaugurated by Dr. Theodor Herzl, the founder of political Zionism, at the first Zionist Congress, convened in Basel. It had been adhered to ever since.

In order to be able to conform to this rule, I hauled out my suit of tails, which I had not worn since my wedding nine years earlier, and had the trousers and jacket let out to fit my increased bulk. They were still too tight but in a pinch could serve the purpose. The only part of the outfit I did not take along was my silk hat. I allowed myself to be persuaded by Claire to wear a fedora. When I presented myself in the large hall, in which the opening session was to be held, I found to my consternation that of all the persons assembled the only ones to wear tails were the chairman and the representative of the Swiss government. As for myself, I was assigned a seat in the section occupied by chalutzim attired in shirts and shorts. I stuck out among these plebeians like a sore thumb in my uncomfortable dress suit and just could not get out fast enough to shed my incongruous uniform and vow to give the informer, who had misled me, a good piece of my mind.

Strassburg Visit

On my way to the congress I had a chance to take off a few days in order to visit Claire's maternal uncle in Strassburg, the capital of Alsace, the province of France that bordered on Switzerland, as well as her Aunt Paulette, who lived in the little town of Merzweiler. They both showered me with their hospitality and made me feel very much at home, Uncle Theo in his spacious modern apartment in one of the better neighborhoods of Strassburg, and Aunt Paulette in her old-fashioned country cottage.

While in Strassburg, which combined French charm with German neatness, I worshipped in the small Orthodox synagogue. But I also made the acquaintance of the sumptuous "Reform" temple. Though its rabbi was not particularly noted for his piety, the prayers recited in this place of worship were, with but slight differences, identical with those current in the Orthodox synagogues. The women were seated in the gallery and the men all wore prayer shawls. The only real deviation from the traditional norm was, as in the Oranienburger Temple of Berlin, the playing of the organ by a non-Jewish organist.

As for the Jewish community of Merzweiler, which at that time still boasted some one hundred families, its members were all of them, without exception, Sabbath observers. Nevertheless Aunt Paulette's father-in-law, a typical Alsatian Jew of the old school, who was never without his skullcap and arba kanfos (four-cornered undergarment with the fringes), complained that Judaism was dying in Merzweiler, and he longed for the return of the good old days when things were different.

XL

Recovery and Growth

I WAS BACK in the United States on September 4. One of the passengers on board the Cunard liner *Olympic*, which took me to New York, was Rabbi Aaron Kotler of Lithuania, the founder of the Beth Medrosh Govohah of Lakewood, New Jersey, a school devoted to postgraduate rabbinical research. He came to be recognized as the outstanding authority on Jewish law in the American rabbinate, with an international reputation.

Our country was, in the fall of that year, thanks in a considerable measure to the energetic steps taken by President Franklin D. Roosevelt, gradually recovering from its depression. Beth Tfiloh's financial situation was beginning to look a little brighter. It had become, even more than before, a veritable beehive of activity. Its Sabbath and holiday services were well attended. The fervor and warmth of the participation of the worshippers in the prayers and the congregational singing fascinated whoever was introduced into its atmosphere. Equally well patronized were the Friday evening forums, at which I alternated with my colleagues whose synagogues were within walking distance and with whom I exchanged pulpits. Occasionally prominent laymen addressed these Friday night gatherings.

The membership of the congregation had by then grown to such an extent that even the additional space provided by the Community Center auditorium, which connected with the main sanctuary by opening the sliding doors that served as a partition, and the seats set up on the balcony did not suffice to take care of the overflow. It became necessary eventually to make arrangements for separate services for adults in the gymnasium and later in the beth Hamedrosh, not to speak of services conducted simultaneously by the Hebrew school for children of school age and teen-agers.

The sisterhood and brotherhood had their many and varied functions, the latter serving as the training ground for congregational leadership. The Chevra Tehillim (psalm-sayers), whose president, I. A. Levin, claimed that it had a direct wire to heaven when it recited psalms for the sick or at the bier of the departed, and the Chevra Kadisha, which occupied itself with the preparation for burial of deceased members and was headed until his demise by the saintly Mr. Louis J. Sachs, had their annual dinners. There were also the Chanukah banquets of the congregation, which always drew a record attendance, and the Purim celebrations, to which added zest was given by the fact that the days of prohibition were a thing of the past.

The gymnasium with its basketball tournaments and other athletic activities was a powerful attraction for the Jewish youth of the neighborhood, many of whom later became affiliated with the congregation. The boy scout and girl scout troops were flourishing. There was an active mixed-young-people's society, some of whose members developed into leaders of the Baltimore Jewish community.

I had a hand in the planning of the programs and was deeply involved in the activities of all these affiliates of my congregation. I had even organized a group of Bar Mitzvah boys, who for quite a number of years met every second Saturday afternoon in my house. They enjoyed immensely the refreshments prepared by Claire and were so smitten with the warmth of her reception and her charm that many of them confessed to me years later, when they were married and had families of their own, that they had a secret "crush" on their rebbetzin.

Introducing Bat Mitzvah

I noticed, however, that while our congregation and I, as its rabbi, had been quite successful in attracting the males, the female half of our youth was neglected. In the Hebrew school the boys outnumbered the girls by a ratio of five to one. Since there was no means for officially marking the becoming of age as women in Israel, of the growing daughters of the members of our congregation, many of them went for their confirmation to congregations in which that was the practice. We would then lose not only them but often their parents as well. How was this trend to be combated?

It was just about that time that my former teacher, Professor

Mordecai M. Kaplan, the founder of the Reconstructionist movement, had conceived of the idea of Bat Mitzvah. In his congregation women were called up to the Torah. This would, of course, have been completely out of the question at Beth Tfiloh. So I bethought myself of an adaptation of the same general principle which would be acceptable to our orientation. I was going to instruct our girls, as they were about to reach the age of adolescence, in their duties as women in Israel. At the conclusion of the term I would have them present a program, which would be a summary of what they had learned. They would, on that occasion, also receive a certificate containing the date of their twelfth birthday, according to the Jewish reckoning, when they were charged with the fulfillment of all the commandments of Judaism pertaining to Jewish women.

In order to implement this plan, I called a meeting in my home of the lay heads of our congregation, the brotherhood, sisterhood, young people's group, as well as the principal of our school. I did this in order to apprise them of what I had in mind and secure their cooperation. The reaction of each and every person that attended was so negative that my scheme seemed doomed. After they were gone, Claire turned to me with the question "What do you propose to do now, Sam?" My reply was, "I am going to go through with it." "Go through with it when everybody is pouring cold water on the idea?" "Yes," I said, "I am going to go through with it, and mark my words, they will all fall in line and do what I ask of them. The only reason for their opposition is lack of imagination. They are reluctant to tackle something that has never been tried and that they fear may not work. It would hurt their pride to be the sponsors of a fiasco. I tell you, however, that it will not be a failure, and once they see the results, they will jump on the bandwagon." To their credit, let it be said that they went along with me and they were not sorry.

I started out with a group of five girls. The first Bat Mitzvah celebration was so enthusiastically received that my annual Bat Mitzvah class grew by leaps and bounds, until, at the peak, no less than eighty-seven were enrolled in it, and it was necessary to divide it into two shifts for sheer lack of space and impossibility of handling all the eighty-seven pupils at one and the same time. The consequence, so far as our congregation was concerned, was that the stampede away from Beth Tfiloh for confirmation was effectively stopped. After a few years the number of girls attending our afternoon Hebrew School equaled that of the boys, not to speak of the day school, which had not yet come into being.

The lesson to be derived from this experience is that a spiritual leader who wishes to accomplish something positive must not allow himself to be dissuaded by the laymen's lack of vision. The Torah would never have become the constitution of the people of Israel if its acceptance had been dependent on a canvass of those to whom it was offered. It had to be imposed upon them, according to our sages, by force.

We had no sooner inaugurated our form of the Bat Mitzvah celebration and the instruction preceding it than all Orthodox congregations in Baltimore, led by English-speaking rabbis, followed suit. It is now a well established and widely accepted practice.

XLI

1935–1937

WHILE ALL THIS was transpiring at home, conditions in the world in general were deteriorating. My father's younger brother, Levi Isaac, who had for ten years occupied in Hamburg the position previously held by my father, shocked by the atrocities against defenseless Jews that he had witnessed in the streets of that city, had moved to Tarnov, Poland, where six years later Hitler caught up with him. He met death together with hundreds of coreligionists who were worshipping in his synagogue which had been put to the torch by representatives of the "master race."

The Fuehrer had recovered from the French for his fellow countrymen the rich industrial Saar region without having to fire a single shot. Drunk with victory, he had no difficulty in passing in November of that year the infamous "Nuremberg laws," which deprived the Jews of Germany not only of their citizenship but of the most elemental rights as human beings. Among world Jewish leaders who moved to the United States from Germany that year was Dr. Nachum Goldmann, the doughty fighter for Jewish rights and founder, shortly before World War Two, of the World Jewish Congress. He had alerted his audiences in our country to the impending catastrophe that was to befall European Jewry, usually opening his remarks with the words, "I have come to disturb your peace of mind." Would that he had been wrong in his predictions!

The year, beginning with Rosh Hashanah of 1935, was a very full one for me. Together with the late Rabbi Edward Israel, who was an ardent Zionist, and Dr. Herman Seidel, the veteran champion of Labor Zionism in Baltimore and the United States, I reported at a joint gathering about the 19th Zionist Congress, which we had attended.

Each of us had a different opinion about the accomplishments of this concourse of world Jewry, according to his particular Zionist orientation, so that one could not blame the chairman for asking, when the meeting was over, what had really happened.

Later on that same year, my first scholarly work since the publication of my doctoral dissertation made its appearance. I did nothing to promote the sale of my *Interpretation of the Bible in the Mishnah* because it seemed to me to be too technical for popular consumption. Nevertheless the brotherhood decided to take cognizance of the event. So Thursday evening, February 21, 1936 was set aside for the purpose. The principal address was delivered by Professor W. F. Albright, chief of the Oriental Seminary of the Johns Hopkins University, with whom I served. My friend and colleague, Rabbi Adolph Coblenz, also spoke, and all present were deeply impressed.

In that same year our first group of B'not Mitzvah made its debut. The girls, who had completed my course and had reached their twelfth birthday, were officially welcomed into the ranks of Jewish womanhood at the morning services held in the synagogue on Saturday, March 14.

In June our Young People's Cultural Group, which had been under my direction, concluded its season of activities with a Palestine program in conjunction with Hapoel Hamizrachi of Baltimore. My Palestine tour, which had been scheduled for that summer, had to be canceled on account of the disturbances in the Jewish homeland instigated by the grand mufti, which made travel in the country unsafe.

Beth Tfiloh's Fifteenth Anniversary

In the fall of 1936 Beth Tfiloh had completed a decade and a half of its existence as a religious congregation. This was most certainly reason for celebration, and celebrate we did. An entire week in the month of December was dedicated to festivities, each presenting a different aspect of the congregation's manifold activities. The first Sunday was devoted to the youth, namely the school and the community center. Wednesday evening was given over to Torah. The principal speaker was Rabbi Ephraim Eliezer Yolles, one of the finest representatives of Chassidic Judaism, a man who combined deep erudition with aristocratic dress and bearing. While my parents were in Europe in the summer of 1923 I had studied Talmud with him in Atlantic City. He is today the nestor of the Orthodox rabbinate of Philadelphia, highly respected by all.

On Thursday evening the playshop of our Community Center,

together with the Young People's Cultural Group, presented dramatic sketches, and an essay contest was held. At the morning services of the anniversary Sabbath following that Thursday, sermons were delivered by my teacher, the venerable Dr. Moses Hyamson, rabbi of the Orach Chaim Congregation of New York, and myself. The Shalosh S'udoth, the third meal eaten on Saturdays between the afternoon and evening services, tendered by the chevrahs, was graced by the participation of Rabbi Jacob Ruderman, founder and dean of the Ner Israel Rabbinical College, which had been established only recently and had during the few years of its existence earned an enviable reputation as an institution for the cultivation of rabbinic lore. He enjoyed international renown, and the relations between him and me have always been most cordial.

The guest speaker at the gala banquet on Sunday was the eloquent Dr. Joseph J. Schwartz, who was to become the chief of all Jewish relief activities in Europe during World War Two and later of the sale of Israel bonds. A son of the revered founder of Baltimore's Talmudical Academy, Rabbi Abraham Nachman Schwartz, he was at the time the executive director of the Brooklyn Federation of Jewish Charities and lecturer in Semitic languages at Long Island University.

Death of Mother-in-law

In March of the year 1937 The grim reaper death again struck in our family. The victim this time was Claire's widowed mother. Elise Woloch was a stunningly beautiful woman. She had borne her widowhood with stoic fortitude. She had a zest for living, and though she had been ailing for a while, she did not allow what she felt inwardly to keep her from attending our Purim play, which was given during the week of her visit in Baltimore. The day after the holiday she returned to New York, and then we received the news that she had suddenly passed away.

It was a severe blow for all of us. We just couldn't believe it was true. After the week of mourning was over, Claire and I decided that while I would be taking care of people who had signed up for my second pilgrimage to the Holy Land during the forthcoming summer, she and our two sons would pay a visit to her mother's family in Alsace. And so it was.

XLII

Second Israel Pilgrimage

THE SHIP THAT TOOK US to Europe was the *Normandie*, the prize of the French Line and the largest passenger boat in the world at the time. It was a floating palace, most luxurious in all its appointments and a pleasure to travel in. Half a mile long from stern to stern, it was so huge that our tiny six-year-old Judah, who liked to go exploring, got lost in it. For a while after our David had called our attention to the fact that his brother was missing, we were frantic, fearing that he might have fallen overboard.

Then, however, I bethought myself that he might have strayed off into the first-class section while the doors between that portion of the ship and ours were still open. So I betook myself to that part of our luxury liner. There I spied in the distance the little fellow, apparently lost, wandering about in utter confusion. "I asked the stewards how I could get back to my mommy," he said in explanation of his disappearance, "but they all spoke French, which I didn't understand, and they couldn't make out what I wanted." From that moment on Judah did not leave us out of sight anymore.

The trip across the Atlantic was very pleasant. The cuisine was excellent. We were served, in addition to the most delicious tidbits, the choicest of Palestine wines. It is no wonder that we quickly acquired unneeded avoirdupoids.

Sleeping Berths

As usual the boat-train that brought us from Le Havre to Paris was several hours late. As a result we missed the express with the sleeping accommodations that had been arranged for by our agent. There was nothing else to do, if we were to catch the Messageries Maritimes liner that was waiting for us at Marseilles for crossing the Mediterranean, than to take the next local with a stopover at Lyons. It had sleeping berths for only eight persons, one compartment being reserved exclusively for men and the other for women. That meant that four of the male members of our group were compelled to spend a virtually sleepless night sitting up in their seats.

Most of our company, which included among others Mr. and Mrs. Abraham Schreter of Baltimore, the Sperlings of Washington, Mr. Simon Needle, the vice-president of my congregation, and Mr. Jacob Miller, president of Baltimore's Mizrachi, accepted the situation sportingly. The only one to complain was an elderly junk dealer from Detroit.

He had never traveled outside of the United States and was furious over having to be separated from his wife for one night. Of course, he held me personally responsible. It was all my fault. He was even more impossible on the train from Cairo to Tel Aviv, when he found that he had been assigned to a second-class coach.

Since on the ships he and his wife occupied first-class cabins, he took it for granted that the same would apply to the railway portion of his trip, even though the instructions given to me as leader of the tour stated otherwise. He refused to accept the explanation that no one in his right senses in Europe or Africa would pay the fare for first class, which was double that of second, when the only difference between the accommodations was one extra seat per compartment, and neither were then air-conditioned and the dust that flew in through the open windows was the same.

Good Riddance

We were glad to be rid of him in Jaffa, where he decided to get off out of fear of the disturbances about which he had heard. We did not see him thereafter.

Notwithstanding the Arab riots of the year previous, which had aimed at disrupting the communications between the Jewish rural settlements and the large centers of population, the Jewish national home had grown in strength as well as numbers. New colonies sprang up overnight. What with the increased aliyah from Germany and other parts of Europe, there was a real burst of activity.

I found in Tel Aviv the son of my father's brother, Levi Isaac, who had just arrived with his bride, another mutual first cousin, the daughter of one of my father's sisters. Moshe Rosenblatt, who had married Regina Rubinfeld, had just been engaged as its cantor by the Ichud Shivat Zion

Congregation, founded by German Jews and one of the leaders of its kind in Israel's largest city. It was a joyous reunion.

We also noted as we visited the already then flourishing Emek (Valley of Esdrelon) the progress made by the kibbutzim of the Hapoel Hamizrachi, which had only three years earlier been struggling for survival.

Breakdown of the Bus

The only incident that might have given us something to worry about, had we been aware of the potential consequences, was the breakdown of our bus outside of Nablus, the ancient Shechem. Our driver turned as white as a sheet when it happened. However, after a two-hour wait, help came from Jerusalem and we were able to proceed. We later learned that if this vehicle had been forced to stay in that hotbed of Arab incendiarism, nothing would have remained of it but ashes.

We spent Tish'ah b'Av, the anniversary of the destruction of the two Temples of Jerusalem, in the Holy City. The new chief rabbi, Dr. Isaac Halevi Herzog, who succeeded Rabbi Kook and who had met my father in Europe, graciously invited me and Claire to have the last meal before the fast and also to break the fast on the night following at his home. I also accompanied him during the day to the Mount of Olives cemetery, where we both prayed at the graves of our respective fathers.

He had a rough time, on account of his doctorate, obtaining the consent to his election to his important post by those elements that were opposed to the heading of Israel's clergy by anyone boasting a university degree. As it was, Rabbi Herzog proved to be a very effective chief rabbi. During World War Two, which was soon to break out, he undertook numerous journeys, at great personal risk, and succeeded, by superhuman effort, in saving countless Jewish lives from certain doom.

Excursion to Switzerland

While I was taking care of my wards in the Land of Israel, Claire and our children were visiting her relatives in France. Left virtually stranded in Paris, because no arrangements had been made for her overnight stay before she could contact her Uncle Theo, she managed by sheer persistence to find quarters. It was not easy because a world's fair was then in progress in the capital of la belle France. The next morning, she and David and Judah proceeded to Alsace. Living for several weeks in the primitive country cottage of a backward Alsatian village was quite an experience for our sophisticated city youngsters. But they were none the worse off for it.

As for Claire, in view of the fact that she was so close to Switzerland, she decided, after having paid her respects to her mother's family, to take a trip to that fabulous vacation country with its bracing atmosphere and its matchless scenery. Uncle Theo was filled with consternation and worry. It seemed to him quite daring for an attractive young woman to travel all alone. "If I had been your husband," he said, "I would never have permitted it." However, Claire assured him that she was well capable of taking care of herself and that nothing that he feared would happen.

So she packed her belongings and off she went. One result of her visit was the discovery of what it meant to be the daughter-in-law of a world celebrity like my father.

Humming Guest

A guest from Hungary in one of the kosher hotels in which she stopped, from the moment that he figured out, by putting together her surname and a few other facts, that she was related to Yossele Rosenblatt, attached himself to her and insisted on her humming for him some of my father's favorite melodies. With French and German, in both of which she was fluent, she made her way around without any difficulty. Total strangers offered help, which she refused in order not to be beholden to them.

Claire also learned, by talking to fellow passengers on the trains in which she traveled, quite a number of whom unsuspectedly turned out to be Jews, how completely unaware these people were of the impending disaster that was to engulf not only European Jewry but every country on that unhappy continent. Her uncles and aunts were certain that they would be left completely unmolested in the event of an invasion of their beloved France.

We in distant American were more apprehensive of what might and did happen than they who lived so close to the volcano that was about to erupt. They were to discover not long after how wrong they had been. But by that time it was too late. They paid for their shortsightedness with their lives. Only Uncle Theo, who had taken the precaution of running away betimes, together with his children, or rather his son—his daughter, Yvonne, was entered for safekeeping in a Catholic convent—survived.

XLIII

Impending Disaster

We had been absent from Baltimore seven whole weeks this time and were glad to be home again. The year 1938 began ominously for the still free, democratic world. In March of that year, Mr. Chamberlain and his French counterpart delivered little Czechoslovakia like a ripe apple into the hands of the power-hungry Adolf Hilter of Germany, hoping thereby to *satisfy* the mad Fuehrer's greed and to secure "peace in our time."

It was a sign of things to come, and set off another scramble on the part of those who read it correctly, to get out of Europe. I sent as many affidavits as were allowed by law to enable relatives in Germany, Poland, and Czechoslovakia to emigrate to places where they would be safe. All I accomplished was to make it possible for some to move to Israel.

I was also successful in receiving, from one of the charitable members of our congregation, a voucher for the maintenance of a beautiful, religious young Jewish woman, whose acquaintance Claire had made in Switzerland. On the basis of that document she was able to enter the United States.

The Crystal Night of November, in the course of which hundreds of the most beautiful Jewish houses of worship in Germany were made level with the gound, including the one in which my father had officiated as cantor in Hamburg, brought a new wave of Jewish refugees to our country.

Among them were two graduates of Würzburg's Jewish Teachers' Seminary. They had been brought over together with others by the Ner

Israel Rabbinical College as students. One of them, whom our neighbor, Mr. George Palmbaum, had introduced to me, started out as a tutor in our Hebrew school. Eric Levi rose in the ranks until, prior to his resignation, he headed our entire educational system. The second, Meir Steinharter, is still today a member of our faculty, and one of the most capable and dedicated pedagogues to be found anywhere. Both have been devoted friends until this day.

The Highways to Perfection II

While these events were taking place, the second volume of my *Highways to Perfection of Abraham Maimonides* was published by the Johns Hopkins Press. It had consumed a great deal of my time and energy. Preparing in duplicate 250 pages of Judeo-Arabic alone by longhand, without the aid of a Hebrew typewriter, was no sinecure. I spent two whole summers and every moment I could snatch from my busy schedule during the rest of the two years on this painstaking task.

It was only the self-sacrifice of Claire, who assumed complete responsibility for raising our children, that made it possible. Absorption in my work took my mind off the summer's heat, which had then not been made bearable by air-conditioning. I always felt that a rabbi should, in addition to the performance of his pastoral duties, make some contribution to Jewish scholarship.

And so long as the members of my congregation were not deprived of my services to them by my preoccupation with what most of them might not even have been able to appreciate or understand, yet gave me tremendous satisfaction, they should not mind. As for myself, the fact that the Jewish learned world took notice of my actions and commended them was compensation enough for my exertions.

Heavy Snowfall

The end of 1938 was followed by one of the severest winters in my recollection. Snow and ice lay on the ground for weeks. On the last Sunday of March, when Claire had already begun to prepare for Passover, the snow was piled almost three feet high. Traffic had come to a virtual standstill. No trolley was running. Cabdrivers refused to go into the sidestreets. Two weddings were supposed to take place in our home that afternoon. The first got started three hours late. The second was two and a half hours behind schedule, and the guests of the second finished the refreshments prepared for the first . In order to make my third engagement in midtown, the only means of transportation available was a grocery truck. It was driven by a member of Beth Tfiloh, and he recognized me as I waited at the intersection of Liberty Heights Avenue and Grantley Road and motioned to him.

Our First Car

Up to that time I owned no automobile. To get to the Johns Hopkins University twice a week I had to use, since there was no direct connection, no less than three streetcars. So long as both my mother and my mother-in-law needed my support, I begrudged myself this luxury. One day our Judah, who was only eight at the time, challenged my logic. If our grocer's clerk could afford a car, he asked, why couldn't I? He was right, so we acquired our first automobile. Its cost was below six hundred dollars. Although I passed ty driving test after several weeks of coaching, I never became what could be called an expert driver. Shortly after obtaining my license I nearly ran up one lamp-post and dented my fender on another. Up to the present, however, my luck has held out. Whatever accidents I had were minor, most of them incurred while backing out of parking lots.

World War Two Begins

In September of the year 1939, Hilter, after swallowing Austria, Czechoslovakia, Danzig and Memel without firing a shot, and immediately upon the conclusion of a nonaggression pact with Stalin, ordered the German Wehrmacht to invade Poland. This started World War Two. For another two years, until the bombing by the Japanese of Pearl Harbor, our nation, although deeply concerned, was not directly involved. It was, therefore, still possible for American Jewry, through the Joint Distribution Committee, to send whatever assistance could be mustered to the stricken Jewish communities of Eastern Europe. But it was not easy. The CARE packages shipped to stave off hunger in Poland and Czechoslovakia were rarely ever delivered to the individuals for whom they were intended. My uncle Samuel Kaufman, the chief cantor of Cracow, had not received the parcels sent by me in response to his frantic appeals to help. The last postcard I had from him, dated January 1941 and bearing the address of his native Brzesko, ended with the words, "we are starving to death." After this all communication with Jews trapped in Hitler-dominated Europe ceased.

XLIV

Life as Usual

WHILE OUR BRETHREN ABROAD, caught in the general upheaval, were going through these convulsions, and we in America, as we read what was happening in Europe, were deeply disturbed, life in our United States, the chief source of supply and the last bastion of hope of the free peoples of the world, continued more or less normally. The time arrived when our oldest son, David, who was approaching his thirteenth birthday, was to celebrate his Bar Mitzvah. Since he had always been an excellent student, a child whom it was a pleasure to teach—he had begun to learn Hebrew when he was but five years old—we should have felt completely at ease about his ability to measure up to what was expected of a rabbi's son. He did remarkably well in reading the pentateuchal lesson and the Haftarah, and his talks in both Hebrew and English at the Kiddush tendered to the congregation were most impressive.

Yet for us, his parents, it was our first such experience, and our nerves were on edge. On the Friday night preceding that Sabbath, neither Claire nor I was able to sleep a wink. We attributed our insomnia to the hardness of the mattress of the beds which our next-door neighbors had put at our disposal, since we had turned over our own bedroom to my mother and stepfather, Dr. Snitzer. She had accepted the proposal of marriage of this East Side Jewish intellectual and Yiddish writer, after years of widowhood, just in order not to burden her children with her needs. The next night we occupied the same beds and had no difficulty sleeping. Our David's Bar Mitzvah, which took place in August, had been the occasion for a marvelous family reunion. In addition to my mother and Dr. Snitzer, all our brothers and sisters and their spouses had come from New York, as well as my boyhood friend George Robinton and his wife, Bea.

Our Heritage

In the fall I had the pleasure of seeing my first collection of sermons, entitled *Our Heritage*, in print. Its reception was such that within a relatively short period of time the entire edition was sold out.

As for the contents of these addresses, which had been delivered by me on the festivals as well as on Sabbath mornings, they were by no means simply exercises in homiletics. I always tried in my preaching to deal with the problems of the hour, never shying away from coming to grips even with the challenge presented to the traditional Jewish viewpoint by the theories of higher Bible criticism.

Hitler Conquers Europe

By the time the year 1940 had come to a close, Hitler's Wehrmacht had conquered not only Poland, Norway, Holland, and Belgium but also France. The British had barely managed to extricate the bulk of their forces from Flanders. Denmark had voluntarily surrendered. London and other cities of Great Britain had been blitzed and severely mauled by the Luftwaffe. In August of 1941 the Germans invaded Russia and moved deep into the heart of that vast country.

Although the prowling in the Atlantic of the German U-boats made the navigation of that ocean by neutrals very difficult, and President Roosevelt had sold the British fifty of our overage warships, we were not yet directly involved in the conflict. Nazi sympathizers were, therefore, free to operate at will in our United States. To offset their anti-Jewish activities in Baltimore, several concerned Jewish leaders of Baltimore, headed by the late Judge Simon E. Sobeloff, organized a Baltimore branch of the American Jewish Congress, which I was to serve as president from 1944 to 1946.

A New School Building

While the lights of the populous and flourishing Jewish communities on the continent of Europe were being extinguished one after another, American Jewry was growing up. Forest Park witnessed an influx of former Jewish residents of East and South Baltimore, and my congregation was the beneficiary. The enrollment of our Hebrew school had increased to such an extent that the classrooms on the second and third floors of our Community Center building above the auditorium no longer sufficed for all its pupils. To meet the needs, the cottage adjacent to the synagogue on Garrison Boulevard was purchased and torn down, and a three-story fireproof building with concrete floors, brick walls, and a stone facade to match our sanctuary was erected on the site. The spearhead of this undertaking was Kabe Millman, who had served as president of Beth Tfiloh, since 1932. A simple, unsophisticated businessman and observant Jew, in whose home Claire and I had conducted the Passover Sedarim when our family was still small (we had alternated between his household and that of the Allens and the Shillmans), he loved his synagogue dearly. Far from being one of the most affluent members of the congregation, Kabe Millman was extremely generous. He had the joy of seeing the new edifice dedicated at a ceremony which took place on September 28, 1941.

It was fortunate that this addition to our complex of buildings was completed when it was, because not long after, on December 7, the attack on Pearl Harbor by the Japanese, whom Hitler had won as an ally, brought us officially into World War Two, and all construction for purposes not connected with the war effort had to come to a halt.

XLV

A Day School at Last

ONCE WE HAD COME into possession of these greatly expanded facilities, our thoughts turned to the realization of a plan I had cherished ever since I had become rabbi of Beth Tfiloh, namely, that of establishing a day school similar to the Talmud Tora Realschule of Hamburg, Germany, in which I had received my early education. By offering instruction in Jewish as well as secular subjects during regular school hours, it would be possible to give the children taking these courses a much more intensive indoctrination in their religious heritage than they could absorb during the six hours a week maximum in afternoon Hebrew schools, when pupils as well as teachers were already exhausted.

The initiative in launching this project was taken by an enterprising young teacher, Eda Bess Krivitsky, who subsequently married Rabbi William Novick of Chicago. With a limited number of five-year-olds she opened a daily Hebrew kindergarten. This was gradually expanded into a full-fledged day school. The man who developed this was an educator by the name of Stanley Ginsburgh, who was to replace Maurice Perman, who had decided to study for a doctorate in psychology and leave the field of Jewish education until he obtained his degree.

Stanley Ginsburgh, Executive Director

In order to find out at the scene of his activities more about the qualifications of Dr. Ginsburgh as both pedagogue and administrator, I was asked to visit the city of Springfield, Massachusetts. I was to gather whatever information I could from a fellow-alumnus, the erudite Rabbi Isaac Klein. The result was that Dr. Ginsburgh, who had been well recommended, was invited, in the fall of 1942, to become not only the principal of our school but the executive director of all other functions of the congregation as well. The truth of the matter is that he was a man who was just brimming over with creative ideas, and was adept besides in implementing them. He was, in other words, a true executive.

The choice of Stanley Ginsburgh as professional coordinator of the farflung activities of our growing congregation contributed in no small measure to its progress in many directions. In addition to playing a major role in enabling me to realize a dream I had cherished ever since I had become rabbi of Beth Tfiloh, namely, that of the establishment of a day school, he was responsible during his tenure of office for many constructive innovations. It was during the six years that he functioned as our executive director, up to the time of his premature death at the age of forty, that the practice was begun of initiating at the synagogue services on Simchat Torah morning the beginners classes of our Hebrew, Sunday, and day schools, which totaled at the peak some 220 youngsters.

It was then that the Saturday preceding Mother's Day was set aside as Mother-Daughter Sabbath, with exercises involving the women, acceptable to a congregation like ours. It was he who called attention to the merits of the Morris Silverman High Holiday prayerbook, which we adopted, supplementing, in a separate pamphlet printed by our congregation, the selections omitted. He prevailed on the lay leaders to print the programs for the special Thanksgiving services, which were compiled jointly by me and him, as well as the cantata I had written for the annual Bat Mitzvah celebrations, and the special services held on such occasions as the death of President Roosevelt and the end of World War Two. He had a knack for securing funds for all kinds of purposes in connection with the operation of the school and community center. Recognizing administrative ability in Howard Shpritz, a teacher who had been with us since his seventeenth birthday, he appointed him educational director of our schools, while Michael Kitt, who taught in the Baltimore public schools, was in charge of the youth and center activities. Our boy and girl scout troops flourished.

New Lay Leaders

In all these matters he enjoyed the encouragement and close collaboration of the enterprising new chairman of the board, Reuben H. Levenson. Reuben was elected in place of Sidney A. Needle, who, after serving for ten years with Kabe Millman, had been appointed judge of the Juvenile Court of Baltimore.

Not the least among the achievements of the new executive director was the arrangement of monthly forums held during the week. They brought to our synagogues such outstanding personalities as the popular columnist Dorothy Thompson; the then senator of Minnesota and later vice-president Hubert Humphrey; Mrs. Franklin D. Roosevelt; Cantor Moshe Kussevitsky; the famous author and critic Ludwig Lewisohn; the distinguished Orientalist, Professor Yahuda; and Dr. Stephen S. Wise, the foremost tribune of American Jewry and the most powerful voice of the American conscience. Many of these celebrities Claire and I had the pleasure to entertain in our home.

To accomplish what he did, Stanley Ginsburgh had to be aggressive, and the tendency of those, who are conscious of the powers they possess is to overreach themselves. This happened in his case also, and it led inevitably to a confrontation between him and me as spiritual leader of the congregation. Fortunately he was intelligent enough to realize when he had made a mistake, and once we had reached an understanding there was no more friction between us. Even though we did not always see eye to eye in religious matters, he recognized that in that field I was the authority. The result was total cooperation regardless of what his personal views might have been.

XLVI

America Joins the War

WHILE THESE DEVELOPMENTS were taking place in my immediate surroundings, the war between Hitler and Japan on the one hand and the free world on the other, as well as the near extermination of the Jews of Europe, was reaching a climax. The toll in human lives lost was stupendous. Beth Tfiloh, too, had its victims, although their number was infinitesimal compared with the losses sustained by the Jewish communities abroad.

Birth of Our Youngest

Somehow or other nature has a way of making up for such casualties by an increase in births. We were blessed, on the eve of the new year of 1943, by the birth of our youngest son, who was named Josef after my father, and Ellis to commemorate his maternal grandmother, Elise.

Little Pet

Just at this time our Judah, who often did the unusual, contracted a habit that had to be broken. We promised him as a reward for his cooperation, a cocker-spaniel, on the acquisition of which he had set his heart. And so I, who was never much of a dog fancier, was charged with the assignment of visiting a number of kennels in the city, until I found the desired pet. It had to be pedigreed according to Judah's specifications since nothing else would have satisfied him. The little dog was brought home, to the child's delight. However, while Judah loved the animal, it was too much trouble for him to housebreak him. With a two-month-old baby in the house and dog of the same age, our sleep at night was often disturbed by a duet between the two.

Collections of Essays

In March of that year, the Behrman Jewish Book House produced my sixth publication, a book of essays entitled *The People of the Book*. It contained, among other things, the lectures I had delivered at the Jewish Theological Seminary in 1933 on "Mohammed's Jewish Teachers." Included also was my paper presented in 1935, the eight hundredth anniversary of the birth of Moses Maimonides, before the Johns Hopkins Institute of the History of Medicine, on the place of that Jewish thinker in the history of philosophy. It was very favorably received. The review featured by the *Baltimore Jewish Times* was written by none other than the sister of Miss Henrietta Szold, Mrs. Benjamin Levin, who was a frequent worshipper in my synagogue. Three years earlier the Mizrachi Organization of America had brought out another volume of my essays under the name, *This Is the Land*. It included a number of addresses dealing with the Jewish homeland and the ideology of Religious Zionism. One of them, a decade before it happened, predicted the inevitability of the emergence of an independent Jewish state.

XLVII

Our Judah's Bar Mitzvah

THE DATE OF THE BAR MITZVAH of our second son, Judah, which was to take place on Saturday, February 19, 1944, was now approaching. Since we expected a lot of out-of-town company, we thought it was time to remodel our kitchen, the renovation of which, long overdue, had had to be postponed on account of the war. But that was easier said than done. There was an acute shortage of materials and an even greater scarcity of artisans to do the work. Finally we got hold of a carpenter who was ready and willing to undertake the job. But when he showed up with his handful of tools, our hearts fell. We wondered whether he was really capable of carrying out the assignment and whether it would be finished in time. To our great joy, and contrary to our doubts, he came through as promised. The day before our guests arrived we had a brand-new kitchen, fully in keeping with what Claire had envisaged.

During the month prior to the completion of the overhaul, our house was in a state of total disarray. The dining and living rooms were filled with furniture. The dishes, which had had to be stacked away, were almost inaccessible, and plaster and debris were everywhere. While she was in the midst of all this mess, Claire received a telephone call from Judah's school that our candidate for Jewish manhood had been hurt and would she come and get him. "Can't you put him into a cab and send him home?" she asked. "I'm just too busy right now." "No, that's impossible. We are afraid he may have broken his leg." So Claire bade our dear family physician, Dr. Kurt Levi, who was always at our beck and call, to make all the necessary arrangements for our son's treatment by a well-known Baltimore orthopedist. Judah, never too easy a lad to handle, tried to tell the doctor, who was not particularly distinguished for patience, how to set the fractured bone. This was the last straw. It almost drove Claire, who had been very much unnerved by the excitement of the immediate past, into hysterics.

All this happened just two and a half weeks before the Sabbath of the Bar Mitzvah. For Judah it was a blessing in disguise. It made it possible for him to devote himself, as he had not done up to that point, to the thorough study of the text of the portion of the week that he was to read in the traditional chant. The result was that in spite of his handicap, with his broken leg in a cast, he performed without a flaw in the synagogue, to which he had had to be carried across the snow and ice by his uncles.

Then came the moment when, in the presence of the overflow crowd of worshippers I had to address my son, as it was my custom to charge all Bar Mitzvahs. Noting that he was swaying, I motioned to him to sit down. However, in the sight of the entire assembly he shook his head in stubborn defiance, so that I was compelled to take hold of him bodily and force him down. Thereafter, so he claimed, he did not hear a word that I was saying. He seemed, however, fully composed when, at the luncheon following the services, he delivered his speeches in Hebrew and English. The latter, he commented, was intended for the benefit of those of his listeners who did not know Hebrew. The explanation, he added, was his own. It had not been authorized by his parents.

XLVIII

Saadia's *Book of Beliefs*

NOT LONG AFTER this family event I received an academic assignment which was one of the greatest compliments ever paid me. Yale University, one of the oldest and most prestigious institutions of higher learning in our United States, had been the recipient of a grant from an American Jewish Maecenas by the name of Louis Rabinowitz for the purpose of publishing translations of Jewish classics not available in the English language. I had long toyed with the idea of doing for the magnum opus of the pioneer of medieval Jewish philosophy, Saadia Gaon, the head of the Babylonian academy of Sura, what Salomon Munk of Paris had accomplished nearly a century earlier for the *Guide of the Perplexed* of Moses Maimonides. Now this very task was thrown into my lap by a group of scholars headed by the late Professor Harry Wolfson of Harvard, the foremost authority in the world on Jewish medieval thought. What was involved was not merely a matter of rendering into English the Arabic original of the *Book of Beliefs and Opinions*. It was necessary to find the modern equivalents of the terminology and concepts prevalent in the tenth century C.E. and make them comprehensible to the average intelligent reader of today. I had to be in possession also of the Arabic text and whatever translations into Hebrew and modern languages were available.

Fortunately for me, a very resourceful Viennese Jewish bookseller who had recently settled in New York, Philipp Feldheim, was able to supply to me all the books that I needed, including the monograph of an English musicologist by the name of Henry George Farmer on Saadia Gaon's theories about "the influence of music." Then, in the summer of

1944, I met, at the Inter-American Jewish Conference convened in Atlantic City by the American Jewish Congress, in which I had played my role in Baltimore, a Rabbi Algazi of Montevideo, Uruguay. He called my attention to a dissertation by his former teacher at the Sorbonne, Rabbi Moise Ventura of Alexandria, Egypt, on the religious philosophy of Saadia Gaon. It took half a year from the time of my order for the volume, which was shipped from Paris, to arrive, stamped "Passed by the board of censors."

My work had reached the finishing stage in 1946, when I learned, to my distress, that a translation into English of Saadia's philosophical masterpiece by a very competent scholar, Dr. Altmann of Manchester, England, had just been issued by the East-West Library. That would have made my translation superfluous, and all my exertions of two summers and every spare moment during the remainder of the two years I had spent on the execution of my assignment would have been for nought. It was my good fortune that the Altmann translation was only an abridged version, whereas mine was complete. Furthermore, I had been asked to prepare a detailed table of contents and an appendix of sixty pages. My edition had, therefore, not forfeited any of its usefulness. Though the stipend I was promised was very modest, the lavish praise I received from Professor Wolfson and other specialists in the field was ample reward for my efforts. In addition, the proposed publication of the volume, the first series of Judaica under the Rabinowitz Foundation to make its appearance, was directly responsible for my promotion to the position of associate professor of Oriental languages at the Johns Hopkins University. This was a distinction conferred on very few practicing rabbis in sole charge of the rabbinical functions of so large and prominent a congregation as Beth Tfiloh was at that time.

Death of President Roosevelt

The ghastly war came to a close in 1945. Before it was over, the man who had been at the helm of America's ship of state longer than any of his predecessors or successors in the presidency, died. Franklin Delano Roosevelt's passing was universally mourned. Like other congregations throughout the country, ours held an impressive memorial service in his honor in its synagogue, which was filled to overflowing for the occasion. Only later was it learned that our idol had clay feet. The great humanitarian, whose heart went out for his fellowmen in need, could have done far more than he did, had he only wanted to, to save from their bitter fate at least a portion of the six million Jews who perished at the hands of Hitler and his henchmen.

In July of that year our David reached his eighteenth birthday. He had by that time completed his college education. He accomplished what normally requires four years in twenty-six months, and had been admitted to Phi Beta Kappa to boot. In order not to be drafted into the army as an ordinary private, he joined the Merchant Marine Cadet Corps, to undergo training that would make him an officer. The school to which he was assigned was the one in San Mateo, California. Little Josef, who was then only two and a half years old, took the departure of his oldest brother so hard that it made him ill for awhile.

Touring the West for Mizrachi

As for me, I decided to make at least one trip to see him. Since I was going to the Far West anyhow, I volunteered to visit on behalf of the Mizrachi Organization, which was so close to my heart, the most important chapters located there, and thus make what contribution I could to the strengthening of the movement.

Of the cities I toured, I found Jewish life best organized in Denver, Colorado, and Seattle, Washington. Even the Conservative congregation in the first, the Beth Hamedrosh Hagodol, which had for more than half a century been served by Rabbi D. E. Hillel Kauvar, was close to Orthodoxy, while the second boasted many individuals who combined wide Jewish learning with sincere piety. The status of Judaism was far less ideal in Portland, Oregon, and in San Francisco, the center at that time of the most radical Reformists, although it had the most magnificent Jewish house of worship in the world. As for the Jewish community of Los Angeles, which was growing so fast that it soon became the second largest in America, it suffered then already from lack of leadership and integration.

XLIX

Rabbinical Problems

UPON MY RETURN HOME I found that the trend toward Conservatism among certain elements of my congregation, which had already manifested itself when I became its spiritual leader, was coming to a head. The demand for changes in the ritual which were contrary to the express provisions of Beth Tfiloh's charter and which, I could not, in good conscience sanction, had become so insistent that as the rabbi of the congregation I had to make my position clear. I was completely in favor of progress, of making use of the most up-to-date methods for enhancing the beauty and decorum of our services and making our worshippers comfortable. That is why I suggested and pressed for the issuance of a Book of Life in connection with our Yizkor service on the Day of Atonement to take the place of the viva voce announcement of memorial offerings. For that reason also I hinted in my Yom Kippur sermon at the installation of air-conditioning, which became a reality two years later.

I could not, however, for the life of me see how such deviations from the norm as mixed seating, syncopation of the traditional prayerbook, and the substitution of English for the original Hebrew text would contribute to the strengthening among young or old of loyalty to Jewish tradition or greater attachment to the beliefs and practices of Judaism. So I took a firm stand against the proposed innovations. The result, as might have been foreseen, was that a number of the affiliates of our congregation, including several of the most affluent and influential, resigned to form a synagogue of their own founded on principles in keeping with their views. I bore them no malice because the differences between us were purely ideological, not at all of a personal nature. We parted good friends. They went their way and the majority that remained continued on the road they had followed theretofore. However, the predictions of those who had warned that without the support of the families that had left, it would be impossible for Beth Tfiloh to carry on, did not come true. On the contrary, notwithstanding the reduction in the numerical size of its membership, our congregation was stronger than ever. Because of the greater homogeneity that had been achieved, and the higher measure of cooperation it was able to count on now that the dissidents had eliminated themselves, it was able to go forward in many directions. It was in a position during the next few years to pay off the remaining indebtedness on its buildings, to remodel the beth hamidrash into a beautiful memorial chapel honoring the sons of Beth Tfiloh who had served in World War Two, and to raise a fund of $100,000, which for fifteen years made up the deficit incurred by the operation of the day school. Last but not least, enough money accumulated from savings set aside during two decades to make it possible to pay cash for the land acquired when the congregation was compelled by circumstances to move from its original home in Forest Park to its present location in Pikesville.

The Question of Kashruth

Another problem that presented itself to me and called for my involvement was the chaotic state of kashruth not only in my own neighborhood but in Baltimore as a whole. There was no guarantee that shops with the Kosher sign on their windows really lived up to their pretensions because there was no means of compelling their owners to have the products they offered for sale inspected. To remedy the situation, after repeated complaints, I set out with the help of a number of interested laymen and rabbis to form a Kashruth Council. Simultaneously therewith the mayor and city council were prevailed upon to pass a kosher food law to protect the public against misrepresentation and fraud. The inspector engaged by the Vaad Hakashruth with the revenue from membership subscriptions and the proceeds of the annual banquet, of which I served as chairman for a full quarter of a century, was armed with the power of the law. Thenceforth edibles advertised as kosher had to comply with the rules or the shops in which they were sold were forced to close or go out of the kosher food business.

L

A Year of Decisions

THE YEAR 1947, which followed, was for me, as well as for world Jewry in general, a year of decision. Early that year I was asked by a delegation of the Shaar Hashomayim Congregation of Montreal, the wealthiest and most prestigious community of Canadian Jewry, with an orientation almost identical with that of Beth Tfiloh, to become its spiritual leader. Rabbi Herman Abramowitz, who had served it with distinction for many years, was no longer able, on account of illness, to carry out his rabbinical duties. Whoever, therefore, would be chosen to take his place would become, upon his demise, his successor. It was a most flattering offer, and a marvelous opportunity for my personal advancement. However I turned it down. One of the reasons was that I had just been notified by Professor Albright of my elevation to the rank of associate professor of Oriental languages at the Johns Hopkins University, and I was most reluctant to sever my connections with this renowned institution of higher learning.

Birth of the State of Israel

On November 29, 1947, the United Nations General Assembly, after hearing the reports of several commissions that had been charged with presenting a practical plan for putting an end to the irreconcilable conflict between the Arab and Jewish communities of Palestine, passed the resolution calling for the establishment, on the portion of the Holy Land west of the Jordan River, of two independent commonwealths, one Jewish and the other Arab.

This resolution was implemented, so far as the Jewish settlement on the soil of Jewry's ancestral homeland was concerned, by Israel's declaration of its independence on May 14, 1948. It was certainly the single most important event in modern Jewish history, putting an end to nearly nineteen centuries of Jewish homelessness. Ours is the generation that had the good fortune to witness what our predecessors had dreamt about but never lived to see realized, namely, the return of sovereignty to the Jewish people after almost two thousand years of subjection to alien rule.

It was an opportunity as well as a challenge. It was an opportunity because from that time on, whatever the difficulties encountered by them were, the Jews became, in their national home at least, masters of their fate. It presented an opportunity for development and growth limited only by their own will and the resources they could muster. But it was also a challenge. It imposed upon Jews everywhere, in the diaspora as well as in the Land of Israel itself, the responsibility of doing whatever was humanly possible to make Israel a viable state, strong enough to withstand the forces that might jeopardize its existence and well-being. Who would have known then that this responsibility would, after more than twenty-seven years of glorious achievements, which fully justified the efforts that went into making the dream of national rebirth come true, be greater than ever before?

Public Sedarim

It was by a very happy and timely coincidence that I prevailed upon my congregation to arrange for the holding in its premises that year of public Sedarim on the first two nights of Passover. My motive in inaugurating such a congregational activity was to make it possible for families that had no one to carry out the inspiring ritual ushering in Israel's ancient freedom festival to render it meaningful. And really, because of the way in which it was organized by us, with the involvement of the youngsters and the participation of all who were present in the selections chanted, the hundreds who availed themselves of this opportunity behaved not like guests in a hotel or spectators at a game. They resembled the members of one large family working in concert and harmony.

For twelve years I led this function all by myself. At the conclusion of this period, I made a recording of the Seder service entitled *This Night Is Different*. I did this as an educational venture enabling families in remote places, far removed from centers of Jewish life, by following the recording, to learn how to proceed at the family meal on the opening nights of Passover.

Saadia Translation Published

At the end of the month that marked Israel's national rebirth, Yale University published my translation of Saadia Gaon's *Book of Beliefs and Opinions*. Due cognizance was given to this event by my congregation in a program in which Dr. Abraham A. Neuman, the eloquent president of the Dropsie College of Hebrew and Cognate Learning, was the principal speaker, and at which Professor W. F. Albright also commented on the significance of this scholarly achievement.

LI

Mission to South America

SHORTLY AFTER this gala evening I left for another mission on behalf of Mizrachi. This time my assignment took me to South America, to the Jewish communities of Argentina, Uruguay, and Brazil. It was a most enlightening, although not uniformly exhilarating, experience.

The tour was for me a real eyeopener. It unfolded to me a world that had theretofore been a complete stranger to me. It enabled me to have a glimpse at the life of my coreligionists who were settled there, their achievements as well as their problems. It also afforded me an opportunity to test my proficiency in languages of which I had up to that time made but little use in public, namely, Yiddish, Spanish, and German.

Buenos Aires

Buenos Aires impressed me as, on the whole, a beautiful city, bearing a striking resemblance to Paris, especially the Teatro Colón, which was in certain respects a replica of the famous Opera. Rio de Janeiro, with its long waterfront against the backdrop of the mountains behind, which necessitated the circling, for at least an hour, of airplanes landing there, was magnificent. São Paulo was fast developing into the number-one metropolis of the South American continent.

The Jewish community of Buenos Aires, which already then counted about a quarter of a million souls, had established a number of fine institutions. The most important was the Sociedad Hebraica. It was an outgrowth of the Hebrew Burial Society, which was organized for the express purpose of keeping the "unclean," the Jewish white-slave traffickers who were Argentina's first Jewish settlers, from being interred in the official Jewish cemetery.

The Sociedad boasted headquarters rising twelve stories high. There were also several flourishing Jewish banks and hospitals, a branch of the World Jewish Congress, a Jewish Mercantile Club, and a sports center. Yet so far as Judaism was concerned, much was left to be desired. The synagogues on Sabbath mornings resembled homes for the aged. Since attendance at the public schools on Saturday had been made compulsory by Peron, young children were completely absent. Most adults, except for the retired, were in their stores, factories, or offices. The only exception to this rule was the house of worship of the Syrian Jews, chiefly from Aleppo. There the youth congregated in large numbers because they received their education in the congregation's Escuela Integral, the only equivalent in Argentina of our Hebrew day schools.

Altogether only a small percentage of the generation that were to become the leaders of the Argentinian Jewry in the future received any kind of Jewish education. The largest Jewish school in Buenos Aires was the Yiddishist Sholom Aleichem Schule. It had a student body of about twelve hundred and excellent physical facilities, including classrooms, a library, and an auditorium. The subjects taught, in addition to the regular secular courses required by the government, were the Yiddish language and literature and Jewish history. However, it was only in the sixth grade that the pupils learned about the festival called Passover and how it was observed.

There were only four rabbis in the whole of Buenos Aires worthy of the title. One was the spiritual leader of the German congregation, a sick and feeble old man. A second was a fine Jewish scholar with a doctorate from Berlin but not a very dominating personality. It was at the home of his in-laws that I was a frequent and welcome guest. The third was the rabbi of the aristocratic Calle Libertad Congregation, which the Orthodox shunned for only one reason, namely, that an organ was played there on the Sabbath by a non-Jewish organist, although never during the "three weeks" of mourning for the destruction of the Temple of Jerusalem.

The fourth was at the time chacham of the Syrian congregation. He was also the president of the local chapter of Mizrachi. He taught me my first lesson in the behind-the-scenes politics that are the ruination of the noblest causes. Instead of assisting me in gaining an entree into circles that could provide the funds so sorely needed to maintain the educational and other institutions of Religious Zionism in the Land of Israel, he put stumbling blocks in my way.

To cite but one example, arrangements had been made, with the help of a prominent member of the Sephardic Jewish community of Buenos Aires, Mr. Elias Teubal, to have me address the Jewish Mercantile Club in Spanish. It would have been quite a sensation, and highly productive so far as the Mizrachi projects in Israel were concerned. Everything was set for my appearance. Invitations had even been sent out. Then, at the last moment, I was informed that the affair had been called off at the instance of the Chacham who, being a comparative newcomer in Argentina, was not yet fluent in the country's vernacular.

Montevideo

I was more fortunate in Montevideo, the capital of the then democratic republic of Uruguay, thanks to the help of a young and enterprising Mizrachi leader who later became the Uruguyan consul in Haifa.

It was in Montevideo that I again met Rabbi Algazi, whose acquaintance I had made at the Inter-American Jewish Conference in Atlantic City several years previously. He was the spiritual leader of the Sephardic congregation, and I had the privilege of speaking at a Friday night service in his synagogue and witnessing there and then a Bar Mitzvah celebration.

In introducing me, my host, under the impression that I would deliver my address in English, requested the part of the audience that would not understand what I had to say, to extend to me the courtesy of sitting quietly while I was speaking. It was, therefore, worth watching his look of amazement when I began my remarks in the Spanish vernacular with a modern Castilian pronunciation.

Brazil

My next stop was Sao Paulo, Brazil. During the eight-hour flight to Sao Paulo, I took along with me a grammar of the Portuguese language, which was the vernacular of Brazil, so as to be able to at least understand what I would hear spoken there. I was entertained in Sao Paulo by the Tepermans, in whose sumptuous home my father had stayed nineteen years earlier while on a concert tour. From them as well as from Rabbi Valt, who was in charge of the local Hebrew day school, I learned about the extent to which corruption was rife among Brazilian government officials. I was also told about the social pressures that had to be employed to extract from the well-to-do members of the Jewish community their fair share of contributions to Israel.

LII

1948–1951

Death of Stanley Ginsburgh

UPON MY RETURN HOME after having been away eight weeks— Claire had not been able to accompany me because our Josef was still too young—I learned to my great sorrow that during my absence Dr. Ginsburgh, Beth Tfiloh's executive and educational director, had suddenly died. His demise was, on account of the responsible position he had held and his deep involvement in our congregational structure, a serious loss. Howard Shpritz, who had been his second in command, had been sufficiently initiated into every facet of our congregational activities to be able to step into his place and carry on where his predecessor had left off.

He brought to his office a dedication coupled with humility and human warmth which made him an ideal public servant, eminently fitted for winning friends for our synagogue and continuing to build up its schools. Our relationship during the years of our association was that of brothers.

Sunday Morning Forums

In the fall of that year, out of a desire to give my parishioners the opportunity to become more thoroughly acquainted with Jewish history and literature, I inaugurated the Sunday morning brotherhood forums. I was able to enlist the active assistance of the then brotherhood president, Ellis Peregoff, who had been a source of encouragement to me in my various scholarly activities. For most of the twenty-five years during which I was in charge, another intellectual of our congregation,

Dr. Emmanuel Kaplan, served as program chairman. These forums are now a well-established Beth Tfiloh institution that has served as a model for other congregations of Baltimore.

Our David's Engagement

The year 1948 ended on a very happy note for our family. It was on Chanukah, the feast of lights, that year, that our oldest son, David, became engaged to his life-partner-to-be, Jaclyn Rivkin.

Mexico

The Mizrachi administration must have been satisfied with the results of my tour of South America because at the end of January of the year 1949 I was sent on a mission of a similar nature to another Latin American country, Mexico, our neighbor directly south of our United States. This time I was accompanied by Claire. Conditions of the still relatively small Jewish community of about 25,000 were much superior to those prevailing among the 400,000 Jews living on the South American continent.

At least eighty-five percent of the Jewish youth attended Jewish day schools of one type or another. The numerically largest was the Yiddish school under the direction of Dr. Golomb. Mizrachi's Yavneh had a student body of close to five hundred. Tarbut, which likewise put emphasis on the study of Hebrew, was of about equal size. The Sephardim, made up of Jews from Aleppo and Turkey, with their own synagogues, each of which was equipped with a mikvah (ritual bath), had their own educational facilities. The secular courses of all these schools were completely maintained and controlled by the government. In return they were compelled to admit a number of non-Jewish pupils so as to be entitled to be considered non-sectarian. All Jewish ritual matters were under the sole jurisdiction of Rabbi Rafalin.

I delivered at least fourteen addresses, most of them in Yiddish and a few in Spanish. The Jewish community of Mexico was most hospitable to us and we made many friends, to some of whom we have remained close to this very day. Our hosts this time, in whose beautiful home we stayed for an entire week, were Simon and Betty Hanan. It so happened that I broke my only pair of glasses one morning. Since I would not have been able, without these spectacles, to read the manuscript of the lecture I was to deliver to a group of women later in the day, my hostess took me to a young optometrist of her acquaintance, who had just graduated from a Philadelphia college of opticians and had the most up-to-date equipment. When he asked me when I wanted the glasses and I answered that I needed them that afternoon, he turned to his assistant and said: "The professor wants his glasses yesterday."

Marriage of David and Jackie

The first marriage of their offspring is always an exciting event for parents. That of David and Jackie, which took place in the summer of 1949, certainly was for us. David had just completed the residence requirements for a doctorate in chemistry from the University of Connecticut. The wedding was performed on the afternoon of August 16 of that year in our synagogue, which was filled to capacity. The entire congregation joined in the festivities. Our rejoicing was completely justified because David and the girl of his choice seemed to be ideally suited to each other, and their union, which has already lasted over a quarter of a century, has been blessed by three sons, who have been a source of pure and unadulterated pleasure to their parents and grandparents.

Time marches on. On October 3, 1951 Claire and I would have been husband and wife for twenty-five years. Since we were married right after Sukkot, our anniversary always fell during the fall holiday season when it was impossible for us to take time out for a vacation.

LIII

Israel in 1951

WE THEREFORE PLANNED our trip, in honor of our silver wedding, to Israel and Europe during the summer preceding that date. We had chosen to revisit the Jewish homeland during a very interesting period of its history. The doors of the little land had just been opened wide to receive Jews anxious to settle there. Immigrants poured in from everywhere at the rate of 200,000 per annum. For lack of suitable accommodations, most of them had to be put up for a while, which for a good many stretched into years, in tents or hastily constructed huts, called maabarot.

In these makeshift homes they literally sweltered in the summer and froze in the wintertime. Things are fortunately quite different now. Newcomers are sent immediately upon arrival into apartments prepared for them. There was also a scarcity not only of food, but of everything. Even people who had resided in the country for a long time were compelled in that era to tighten their belts and observe the strictest austerity. Of all this we tourists, whom the government tried to spare the inconveniences, got a taste only when we visited relatives who had been lucky enough to escape from Hitler by taking refuge, when it was still possible, in what was to become the Jewish national home.

The time of this pilgrimage of ours to Israel coincided with the convening of the first Zionist Congress to meet on the soil of the reborn Jewish national home. Mizrachi had just published my brief *History of the Mizrachi Movement*. I was, therefore, considered well qualified to serve as one of its delegates.

The sessions were held in what is now the largest auditorium in

Jerusalem with the finest acoustics, the Binyeney Ha'umah, located not far from the Mosad Harav Kook. A week before the projected opening of the conclave, only a shell of the edifice was completed. The grounds were still unpaved. One wondered whether the building would be fit for use on the scheduled date.

But leave it to the Israelis. When something has to be finished at a certain time, they usually manage to do it. On the morning set for the beginning of the deliberations, the walls were attractively covered by reams of bright fabrics hiding all the rough spots. It was a thrill to listen to the addresses of the members of the government of the first independent Jewish state in nineteen centuries, and to have a share in the resolutions passed for the purpose of coping with the mountainous problems that beset the young republic.

At the same time I was deeply disturbed by the actions of its bureaucracy. I recall distinctly the despair of dedicated people, anxious to establish in Israel industries that would have given employment to thousands, who were prevented from going through with their plans by obstreperous officials. The would-be entrepreneurs were sent from pillar to post as they tried to obtain the necessary permits, until they finally gave up in disgust. I hope this situation has since been remedied.

On the Way to Israel

On the way to Israel we spent several days in Rome, Italy. It was our second visit. A former pupil of mine at the Johns Hopkins University, who held a position in the famous Vatican Library, had promised me that if I ever chanced to come to this seat of the papacy, he would arrange for me an audience with the pope. The invitation had not come through until the last day of our stay, when Claire was busy packing our purchases. Much as I would have wanted her to accompany me, I was compelled to go by myself to the summer home of the head of Catholic Christendom, the Castel Gandolfo, perched high on the hills overlooking Rome. I went out of curiosity, because I was no admirer of his Holiness, who had not exerted himself too much to save even the Jews under his personal jurisdiction and control from the hands of Hitler.

When it was my turn, among some hundred persons assembled in the reception hall for the Udienza Speziale, to exchange a few words with the gaunt, ascetic-looking, black-robed Pius V, I addressed him in Italian to display my knowledge of that language. He answered me in flawless English. What a blow that was to my vanity!

From Italy we flew to Athens, Greece, which had then not yet had a chance to clear away the rubble and ruins left by the devastation of World War Two. We were the guests of a former pupil of our school. As an officer of the U.S. Public Health Service, he had organized a large number of hospitals in various countries of the world.

Sheldon Miller was still a bachelor in his early thirties. Around him revolved the entire Jewish life of the community of fifteen hundred. He was friendly with the king and queen, whom he considered very democratic. We know differently now. His specialty was diet. Since meat was hard to obtain and he could not depend on his help, he served nothing but dairy in his home. He was a marvelous host. Besides offering us his wonderful hospitality, he also provided us, during the three days of our stay with him, with a tour of the historic sites of this most highly developed center, in classic antiquity, of civilization and culture. It included a concert in the open-air theatre of Herod Atticus.

LIV

A Week in Morocco

ON THE WAY HOME from Israel, which was via Paris, Claire elected to go to England, while I proceeded to Morocco. That country, at the western tip of North Africa, had, among the Arabic-speaking Moslem states, the largest Jewish population. It was from there that most of the Oriental Jews who migrated to Israel originated. I was anxious to find out for myself how they were situated in their home country, what their background and their beliefs and practices were, and how they could best be integrated into the society of the Jewish national home once they settled there.

During the week I spent there, I had a chance to make the acquaintance of six Jewish communities. They were those of Rabat, the capital and seat of government, Casablanca, the chief seaport and largest city; Fés, the medieval cultural center; Meknés, the wealthiest; Azemour, the home of a saint; and Sefrou. My guide was an agent of the Joint Distribution Committee, which Mr. Joseph Meyerhoff of Baltimore, already one of the leading American Jewish philanthropists, had contacted. After the closing of the internment camps in Europe, the JDC moved most of its personnel to North Africa, where they were very much needed and could render the most effective services in rehabilitating the neglected Jewish masses.

I had always thought very highly of the work of rescue done by this splendid organization. My respect for it was enhanced by what I was able to see at first hand in Morocco.

The poverty and living conditions of the overwhelming majority of the 300,000 Jews then inhabiting that country, where they were at best treated as only second-class citizens, was unspeakable. Nine out of ten children born never reached their first birthday. Of those that did, many grew to maturity afflicted by all kinds of diseases. Thanks to one decent meal a day and the medical care supplied by the JDC, eighty percent were nursed back to health. The Alliance schools, which have been nationalized since the termination of the French protectorate over Morocco, taught thousands of the Moroccan Jewish youth a trade. The Ozar Hatorah, which replaced the old-fashioned unsanitary chadarim, in which two hundred children would be crowded into a room that would normally accommodate only fifty, achieved excellent results in their Jewish education.

As a whole, Moroccan Jewry was deeply steeped in tradition, with no small admixture of superstition. All Jewish restaurants in Casablanca were strictly kosher. The only question was about their safety from the health standpoint. Because I had not been sufficiently careful, I developed such an acute case of stomach upset that it was only by a miracle that I survived.

I had an opportunity to meet in Meknés the students of the one-year-old yeshivah founded there by the Liubavitch Chassidim, and examine several classes of the large Talmud Torah school that were taught the Bible in Hebrew.

I also listened to a lecture in Talmud given by the learned Rabbi Obadiah of Sefrou, and was the guest in the home of the spiritual leader of Fés on a Friday night. I delivered an address in the synagogue of the latter the next morning in Hebrew, which nearly all the male worshippers, dressed in typical Arab garb, seemed to understand. I was also invited for a meal in the luxurious villa in the Casablanca suburbs by M. Benazeraf, the tea king of Morocco. M. Benazeraf, editor of the French-Jewish weekly of Moroccan Jewry, was the only Jewish member of the Moroccan parliament. He had a perfect command of Hebrew, Arabic, French, and Spanish. He possessed the most complete collection of printed books and manuscripts bearing on the history of the Jews of Morocco. As soon as the Moroccans secured their independence, he was compelled to move to France.

Back in Paris I was eager to find out what happened to the Moroccan Jewish teenagers when they were sent to the Hachsharah camps in preparation for their settlement under the Youth Aliyah program in Israel. To my great dismay, I learned that most of the youngsters, who had been raised in the strictest religious surroundings, shed their habits once they had left home. The boys discarded their tefillin. Both they and the girls disregarded the dietary laws and no longer observed the

Sabbath. When I inquired how this came about, the answer I received was that the counselors sent from Israel had told their wards that in the Jewish homeland these marks of Jewish identity were unnecessary. My complaint about the outrage done thereby to the convictions of the trusting parents of these children, elicited the explanation that it was all due to the insufficiency of religious counselors. Hadassah would have been perfectly willing to make use of such youth directors if only Mizrachi and Agudat Israel would have supplied them. But they didn't. It was by default that the Youth Aliyah officials were compelled to accept what was available.

Beth Tfiloh Day Camp

When I came home to Baltimore, I was delighted to note that the day camp, acquired by my congregation in 1950 thanks to the alertness of people interested in the youth like Al Cheslock, had been put into condition to be used by several hundred youngsters. What some of them learned informally during the two summer months aroused enough of an appetite for Jewish studies in some of the parents as to induce them to enroll their children of school age in our day school.

LV

Beth Tfiloh Celebrates My Silver Jubilee

THE RABBINATE IS CERTAINLY not the easiest or most carefree of professions. It is impossible for a rabbi, if he is a man of principle and a person with strong convictions, to please everybody. Hence the heartaches that must be endured by even the most compassionate and understanding of spiritual leaders, who wants to do what is right by all the members of his flock. However these inevitable minuses are more than compensated for by the marks of friendship shown and the cooperation secured from many of those he has tried to serve. This was demonstrated to me when Beth Tfiloh decided to celebrate the twenty-fifth anniversary of my engagement as its rabbi.

The time chosen for the event was the weekend of June 6, 7, and 8 of the year 1952. My brother-in-law, Rabbi Max Hoch, who had married Claire's youngest sister, Gladys, delivered the sermon in the synagogue on Saturday morning, and our three sons read the Torah. Rabbi Ruderman, dean of the Ner Israel Rabbinical College, spoke at the Shalosh S'udoth meal tendered by the chevrot. My closest classmate and colleague, Rabbi Simon Greenberg, was the guest speaker at the gala banquet held at the Lord Baltimore Hotel on Sunday evening, at which my brother Henry, as well as our choral society, directed by Cantor Kotlowitz, sang appropriate selections. It was a most festive affair, in the arrangement and conduct of which all the officials of the congregation were involved.

An indication of the impression upon all who participated is given by the reflections of a former president of our sisterhood, Bessie Fishman, which were published in the June 20 issue of the Beth Tfiloh Bulletin.

Just as the congregational singing resounded tumultuously, at the Rabbi's Sabbath morning service so must the emotions have been tumbling one upon the other in the hearts of Rabbi and Claire Rosenblatt.

The great joy of gratification emanated from them, and seemed to enter into our hearts—the 1000 people who assembled to do him just honor on that morning.

As David, Judah and Joseph participated in the services, the hearts of their parents swelled with pride and if the tears automatically came forth, no one was surprised—for we all felt the same, and shed a tear of joy with them.

Saturday afternoon, from Minchah time until late into the evening, a well attended Shalosh S'udoth was held.

As an added feature the Youth Mishnayes Class, 9 children, 12 to 14 years of age, presented to the audience a sample of what they have been studying Saturday afternoon during the winter school season.

Now about Sunday.

It was as though each man and each woman were having a "Simcha" of their own. The aura that surrounds the hosts at their own affair was multiplied 750 times. There was a warmth, there was an excitement that permeated the entire hall. Everyone was attired festively, just as though they each were hosts at this most magnificent of affairs. It was something so rare—this outpouring of people to bring to one man so much love, devotion and admiration.

The tributes paid to our beloved Rabbi by the Rabbinate, by our lay leaders, by the Sisterhood and by the Brotherhood, were genuine and sincere. The Rabbi's brother sang. The Choral Group sang, and they have never been so good. The installation of the new officers was excellently executed.

A tiered Birthday Cake was rolled into the room as a special song was sung to him by the Choral Group.

If you have felt the excitement as I write this, it is only a fraction of what really took place. Indeed words are inadequate to catch all of the emotions.

However, of all the tributes of which I was the recipient, in words as well as in the letters that were presented to me, together with a twenty-fifth anniversary volume, none was more gratifying than the following lines written for the occasion by my oldest son, David.

> There is a pride that rightly holds the heart.
> There is a pride that keeps no man apart,
> A pride that binds all whom with love it fills,
> This pride I feel, and you it also thrills.
>
> I speak of one whose ever gentle hand
> Has raised itself to lead and to command,

Whose voice has thundered forth among the great,
And, though it would persuade, would not intimidate;

I speak of one whose wisdom is so deep
That scholars come from far, its fruits to reap—
Yet he, with kindly smile and patience rare,
Instructs young children with full tender care.

This man whose memory is oh so keen
Remembers not the vile, the base, the mean—
No words of anger or reproach come forth.
His instruments are thoughts and deeds of worth.
In principles and God he puts his trust,
Loves not the less mankind who are but dust.

This pride in him I share with you and you,
In him like whom there are so precious few—
And yet I love him more than others can,
For though their teacher, Rabbi, yes, and man,
To whom they all can look with fondness rare,
To me he's these and more they cannot share—
  He is my father.

LVI

For the Sake of Israel

THROUGHOUT MY RABBINICAL career, I had given precedence above other matters to the needs of my congregation and its constituents. Yet I never limited myself to the performance of strictly pastoral duties and preaching. I felt that every Jewish spiritual leader had the obligation to use his influence in furthering the interests of the Jewish people in general and the advancement of Jewish knowledge. This was the reason for my continued teaching at the Johns Hopkins University, my writing and my involvement in Jewish defense organizations like the American Jewish Congress and B'nai Brith. It was responsible for my participation in the work of the National Conference of Christians and Jews and other efforts to foster interfaith goodwill. Above all, however, did it stimulate my interest in Israel.

When, therefore, early in the year 1952 Prime Minister Ben-Gurion, during his visit to the United States, proposed the sale of Israel bonds as a means for the development of the economy of the Jewish homeland, I decided to lend my full support to this project. I discussed the methods of procedure that would produce the best results with several Zionist leaders of Baltimore. One of them was Adolph (Murph) Hamburger. He was then among the few natives of Baltimore of German Jewish descent to participate wholeheartedly in the Zionist movement. He carried weight in the community because of the prestige of his family and his personal integrity. Modest, unassuming, he was a highly cultured man of the world, upon whose brow was written true nobility. What a pity that this dedicated lover of Zion is no longer in our midst, especially now, when his inspiration is so sorely needed!

We came to the conclusion that the time of the year most propitious for a successful campaign was the High Holidays. Especially on the evening ushering in the Day of Atonement, when synagogues had the largest attendance, were the hearts of Jews most responsive to appeals for Jewish causes. But how could one inject into the services of that most sacred night of the Jewish year so commercial a note as that of the lending of money, even if it be to Israel, without disturbing the solemnity of the occasion? I assured Murph that it could be done. All that was necessary was to gear the Yom Kippur message, which is usually delivered shortly after Kol Nidrei, so that it would lead directly into modern Jewry's duties toward the reborn Jewish national home. Immediately after the rabbi's address, the worshippers would be asked to turn down the tabs on the cards they would find on their seats, inscribed with their names and addresses, indicating the denomination of the bonds they were going to acquire. It would take perhaps five minutes, so that there would be hardly any disruption of the service. With the blessing of the board of my congregation I tried this out on the night of Yom Kippur of the year 1952. Without loss of dignity to our prayers, $100,000 worth of Israel bonds, which was then a substantial sum of money, was subscribed to in record time. Our congregation had shown the way. The Orthodox synagogues of Baltimore soon followed suit. Eventually others, including the Reform congregations, came along. I continued making these Kol Nidrei night appeals for the next twenty years, and my congregation responded nobly. My addresses were incorporated in my collection of sermons entitled *Hear O Israel*.

LVII

Yossele Rosenblatt

BEFORE THIS APPEARED in print, I was busy with producing another of a more popular nature. It was the biography of my father, *Yossele Rosenblatt*. The fact is that I had planned to write the story of his unusual and interesting career shortly after his untimely demise. However, since my brother Leo, who had been his business manager and was in possession of most of the details, had expressed a desire to carry out this labor of love, I left it to him. Unfortunately, Leo died at the age of forty-six without having realized his ambition. The task, therefore, devolved upon me. It took me the better part of two years to go through and arrange in chronological order something like ten thousand newspaper clippings, which Leo's widow, Doris, made available to me. The information they contained was supplemented by my father's own memoirs of the early years of his life, published in the Yiddish daily of New York, the *Day*. To this I added the historical background. When, after weeding out whatever seemed repetitious, I felt that my manuscript was in satisfactory shape, I presented it for publication to Farrar, Straus and Young, a reputable New York firm with a following. They agreed to do the job, and when the finished product appeared in the spring of 1954, it was accorded a very warm reception. Favorably reviewed in many periodicals, it was published several years later in a somewhat abridged Hebrew translation in Israel, where it aroused particular interest and was widely read.

On June 11 of the year in which *Yossele Rosenblatt* saw the light of day, I was granted my first opportunity to open a session of the U.S. Congress with prayer. It was followed by two other such functions, one at the suggestion of Congressman Friedel, the other at the instance of a former colleague on the Hopkins faculty, Congressman Clarence D. Long. But of course, the first such experience is always the most thrilling.

LVIII

For Bar-Ilan University

SEVERAL MONTHS LATER, on the evening of November 22, I was presiding in Annapolis, Maryland, at a dinner given on behalf of the second school of higher learning to be founded in Israel. It had long been the dream of Dr. Pinchas Churgin, the successor of Mr. Leon Gelman as president of the American Mizrachi, to build in the Jewish homeland a university with an outspokenly religious orientation, bearing the name of the great Mizrachi ideologist, orator and publicist Rabbi Meir Bar-Ilan (Berlin). I remember accompanying Dr. Churgin, who had for many years been a member of the faculty of Yeshiva University and a highly respected scholar, when in 1951 he and other Mizrachi leaders applied to the prime minister of Israel for a parcel of Jewish National Fund land upon which to erect the buildings of the contemplated institution. Mr. Ben-Gurion, who was not a religiously observant Jew, did not appear to be overly enthusiastic. "What need" he asked, "is there in a little country like ours for another college of the type you are proposing when we have the Hebrew University? And besides, religion and science do not mix." However, our people were persistent, and so they finally got what they wanted. Now the dream of Dr. Churgin, and of others who could see no contradiction between adherence to Jewish tradition and the cultivation of general knowledge, was about to become reality. The construction of the most essential buildings of Bar-Ilan had advanced sufficiently for the institution to open its doors in the fall of 1955, and I was invited by the chancellor to help him screen the first applicants anxious to be enrolled as students.

Dinner at the Governor's Mansion

In order not to come to Israel empty-handed, I organized a committee

Beth Tfiloh at Garrison Boulevard Baltimore, Maryland 1927-1966

Samuel and Claire Rosenblatt about to leave for Israel to dedicate Bar-Ilan University in 1955

of donors and solicitors of funds. It was headed by a close personal friend and generous patron of Jewish institutions of learning in the United States and elsewhere, Philip Needle. Governor McKeldin, at whose swearing in as chief executive of Maryland I had twice been asked to deliver the invocation, put at our disposal the governors' mansion. The banquet was a huge moral as well as financial success. I was able to bring along with me some of "the flour without which there is no Torah" when I arrived in Tel Aviv to assume my duties as the assistant to Dr. Churgin.

Three Months in Israel

My congregation generously granted me a leave of absence of three months. The time I was thereby able to spend in Israel was most rewarding. It afforded me an opportunity to note the progress that had been made by the Jewish national home in the four years since I had been there last. I was delighted to learn that there was now an abundance of food and that my relatives had worked themselves up enough economically to afford apartments of their own. It was a joy to join them in family celebrations like Bar Mitzvahs and weddings. I was also granted the privilege of delivering sermons on Sabbath mornings in the largest synagogues of Tel Aviv and Haifa. The warm welcome I was given proved to me the need, which existed in Israel then and still exists today, for preachers who would speak to the worshippers in a literary Hebrew and deal with topics of current interest.

I had taken along with me to Israel our Josef. He was then twelve and a half years old. I had hoped that by spending a summer in Kfar Batya, the model children's village established by the Mizrachi Women of America near Raanana, he might become fluent in spoken Hebrew. To my disappointment he selected as his roommate and closest pal a chocolate-colored boy from India, with whom he would converse in English. Yet despite the fact that linguistics was not Josef's forte, something did rub off. For when, in the spring of 1974, he revisited Israel as the member of a Young Leadership mission from Baltimore, he was himself most agreeably surprised at the ease with which what he had picked up nineteen years earlier had come back to him and how well he was able to make himself understood.

One thing Josef had never gotten used to was the food served at Kfar Batya. By the time his mother, after spending six weeks traveling through Europe in the company of Mrs. Yoffe, "the mother of Beth Tfiloh," joined us in Israel, he had grown so thin that Claire, deeply disturbed by his loss of weight, immediately took him to a physician for a check-up. After giving him a thorough examination, the doctor assured Claire that her son was in perfect health and still not underweight.

Towards the end of our stay in Tel Aviv, yielding to the earnest pleading of my cousin Regina, whose husband, Moshe Rosenblatt, was in the States looking for a position as cantor, we decided to spend a few days in her ground-floor flat in order to relieve her loneliness. The nights are often hot in Tel Aviv in the summer. Claire, being a lover of fresh air, opened the shutters before going to bed. This almost drove our hostess to distraction. "What are you doing?" she said. "Tel Aviv isn't anymore what it was before the state had come into being. The number of break-ins has increased enormously. You have to be careful!" "But what do you have here that the burglars would want to steal?" asked Claire. "True" replied Regina, "I don't have anything worth taking. But they don't know it."

Dedication

The dedication of Bar-Ilan University took place on one of the hottest days in August. The sun was beating down mercilessly on the people assembled on the campus without shelters overhead. Never in my life was I as uncomfortable as I was that afternoon, covered as I was by my full-length academic black robe. To make matters worse, some of the speakers, instead of adhering to their assigned time schedule, droned on endlessly. One woman, in lieu of a short greeting on behalf of her organization, was so lengthy in her remarks as to evoke the comment by our Josef in his letter to his brothers: "A lady spoke for twenty minutes off the subject." Her performance could not have been more accurately characterized than by this terse description.

On our way back to the States we visited several cities in the north of Italy. We covered so much mileage in Milan, looking for the only kosher restaurant, that when we finally got there, completely exhausted, Josef remarked: "After the food I went without in Kfar Batya, and the marching in Milan, I feel fully conditioned for the army."

LIX

Family Joys and Cares

THE YEAR 1956 was one of joyous family events. Our Josef celebrated his Bar Mitzvah on the first Saturday in January. Like his older brothers he read the entire pentateuchal portion as well as the Haftarah. He acquitted himself in such a manner that his parents and other relatives were mighty proud of him. On June 12 our second son, Judah, was married to Lisa Herzfeld of New York in our synagogue. The wedding was a sort of repeat performance of that of our David seven years earlier. Lisa and Judah had a great deal in common. This included mathematics, music, and bridge. They are, indeed, well matched and have worked together as a team until this day.

Eleven weeks later, on August 31, one week before Rosh Hashanah, our first grandson, Jonathan Israel, our David and Jackie's oldest, was born. His initiation into the Covenant of Abraham took place in our home on the second day of the Jewish New Year festival. This was followed in March by the birth of his cousin, Daniel Isaac, the son of our Judah and Lisa. The day of the circumcision of this second grandson of ours was a hectic one. Yet it ended well and, after all, that is what counts.

To Seattle

For that summer Judah had accepted a position with the Boeing Aircraft Corporation in Seattle, Washington. So he and Lisa put their three-month-old baby into their jalopy and off they drove to the city that was to be their home for three months. When more than a week had passed without a word from them, both we and Lisa's parents became alarmed. The information we received about the nature of the mountain roads over which they had to travel, made us even more apprehensive. Our imagination conjured up scenes of wrecks of automobiles at the bottom of the Sierras with unidentified bodies. In desperation remembering that Judah had grown up in the house of a rabbi to whom people often turned for advice in their distress, I decided to call Rabbi Appel, whom I had met in Seattle in 1946. It was a stab in the dark, one chance in a million. To our most pleasant surprise, the rabbi not only had been contacted by Judah, but Judah, Lisa, and Daniel were in his home at that very moment. What had happened was that Judah had had difficulty in finding quarters, and while he was waiting for an apartment to be readied for him, the good rabbi, though he had six children of his own, put him and Lisa and Danny up in his residence.

Judah's being so far away was an excellent reason for a visit by myself and Claire of the Far West. It afforded us an opportunity to see with our own eyes some of the natural beauties of our country, such as Mt. Rainier in the state of Washington, and Yosemite, with its giant redwood trees, in California. It was also a chance to renew old friendships, such as that of the Karasiks in San Francisco and the Bassans of Beverly Hills. From Los Angeles we proceeded to Denver, Colorado, where we boarded our plane heading for Baltimore.

New Excitement

We had hardly had a chance to rest up from our trip when excitement was in store for us again, and once more Judah was the cause. While motoring with his little family through Yellowstone Park he suddenly became ill. Lisa barely managed to drive him to a hospital in Montpelier, Idaho. His pain was diagnosed as being due to appendicitis, and he was about to have his appendix cut out when his father-in-law, Dr. Herzfeld, who had been contacted in New York, advised waiting until he could make a personal diagnosis on the spot. He arrived in Montpelier by plane the next day. In the interim Judah's bloodcount had gone down and he was in good enough condition to fly to Baltimore to be operated, if necessary, in a hospital with much better facilities than the one in Montpelier. While Dr. Herzfeld took the baby with him to New York, Claire flew to Montpelier, despite the fact that it was just a week before the High Holidays, so that Lisa would not be compelled to drive their car and the trailer, attached to it, all alone to their home at the time in Lafayette, Indiana. When Judah was examined by our family physician in Baltimore, he had so completely recovered from his indisposition that surgery, with all the attending hazards, was completely ruled out. He was able to travel to New York all by himself, pick up his little son, and return to Lafayette, where Lisa awaited him and their Daniel.

Rosenblatt Memorial Concerts

In June 1958, a quarter of a century had rolled by since my father's passing. The 25th anniversary of his death was marked by a series of memorial concerts, beginning with the one in my own Beth Tfiloh, with the participation of the then leading cantor in the world, Moshe Kussevitsky. This function was followed by other such events in New York, Chicago, Montreal, and Philadelphia, all of which I attended.

In anticipation of these memorials, I had prevailed upon the RCA Victor Company to reproduce several albums of my father's most famous recordings, for which I supplied the translation and explanatory notes.

A month after the memorial concert in our home city, our third grandson, Aaron Abel, David and Jackie's second child made his appearance. His anticipated birth made us spend that summer at home.

LX

At the Peak

BY 1959 I HAD for several years been president of the Baltimore Board of Rabbis, which I headed for a full decade and a half. I had organized this body because I was convinced that the advantages to be derived from the cooperation in mutual respect of all members of the rabbinical profession, notwithstanding the differences among them of belief and practice, far outweighed the disadvantages. I never permitted anyone to dissuade me from attending the installation of non-Orthodox colleagues. Thanks to the rapport which I enjoyed with the non-Orthodox as well as the Orthodox, I had an entree to all circles of Baltimore Jewry. This enabled me to be instrumental in saving from demolition the oldest Jewish house of worship in our city and the third oldest in the United States, the synagogue on Lloyd Street built by the Baltimore Hebrew Congregation in 1840. Thanks to my intercession its restoration was made possible; and it is now a Jewish museum in the custody of the Maryland Jewish Historical Society.

While the negotiations for the acquisition and renovation of the old Jewish landmark were going on, important developments took place in Beth Tfiloh. By 1955 the congregation had reached the peak of its numerical growth as well as the extent of its activities. Four separate adult services were conducted in its premises on the High Holidays. The total number of worshippers, including the members of the junior congregation under the direct supervision of the schools, exceeded three thousand. Eighty-seven girls were enrolled in the Bat Mitzvah class which I taught. The number of pupils attending our schools had attained a record high of 1150, which included 350 registered in the day school.

There were two separate principals for the different departments of our school system. Eric Levi, who had a talent for handling masses of children, was in charge of the Hebrew and Sunday schools, while Dr. Meyer Cohen, an able Hebraist, headed the day school. In addition the resourceful Henry Hyman, educational director, made his influence felt in the summer day camp as well as the community center with its numerous clubs, including the AZA units and the boy and girl scout troops.

However, soon after the year 1955, the population of both our congregation as well as of the schools commenced to taper off. The chief reason was one of those phenomena that have been characteristic of nearly all cities, large or small, of our United States. Whether they were impelled by growing affluence or the fact that on account of the marriage of their children, the large homes in which they lived in Forest Park were no longer needed by them and had become too much to take care of besides, people began to move out of the neighborhood. Some joined synagogues in their vicinity and found it more convenient to send their children to schools nearby rather than have them travel long distances. I was afraid that if this trend continued—and it did—a time would come when there would be nothing left of Beth Tfiloh, and all its achievements in the past would be but a memory.

Relocation Becomes Imperative

The leaders of Beth Tfiloh were fully aware of what was happening. They realized that something would have to be done to enable our congregation and its schools to survive. But when they thought of the cost of building, and, what was even more important, of the upkeep, they became genuinely frightened. It took a lot of persuading on my part before a decision to look for a new location was reached. Option after option presented itself, only to be passed up because our people were unable to make up their minds.

When finally they did, other questions had to be answered. Where shall we build? What is available in that particular area? What means do we have to pay for the land? What are our building needs? Who shall be the architect? How will the construction be financed? What will be the fate of our old headquarters in Forest Park?

The undertaking of what turned out to be a gigantic task and its successful conclusion involved the cooperation, the thinking, and the energies of many dedicated men and women. It taxed the generosity of hundreds of loyal Beth Tfilohites. It goes without saying that in most of these operations, I, as befits the congregation's spiritual leader, played a vital role. It was I who was consulted by Zandy Leaderman before he approached the owners of the site upon which our present complex of buildings is situated. It was the nest egg put aside for Beth Tfiloh by my dear friend Simon L. Bank, as the congregation's controller, that made it possible to pay for the land acquired in cash. It was I who helped the architect, Morris Lapidus, design the front of the synagogue, including the choir pit.

It was in my home that the first big gifts' meeting, led by the contributions of the Epsteins, was held. It was to me that the Tuvins first communicated the announcement of their donation, and through me that the memorial in honor of Stanley Sagner was set up by his family. Many of my personal visits resulted in sizable contributions toward the total raised by the building fund committee headed by Louis J. Sagner. It was with me that Ellis Peregoff discussed the ways and means of disposing of our synagogue in Forest Park in compliance with Jewish law. Last but not least, when the time came to apply for the permit to build the apartment units on the congregation property, so that families that wished to live within walking distance of the synagogue could do so, it was my testimony before the zoning commission that was crucial.

All this took time and effort. Ten whole years rolled by from the moment when the fifty-eight acres acquired from the Shriver family were secured and the last portion of the garden-type apartments erected by Gordon Sugar on this property was completed, and it was only after a successful three-year battle in the courts that the foundations of the first units could be laid. The transition cost our congregation twenty-five percent of its membership. It was only gradually that this loss was made up. However, before it was even possible to start looking for a new site, it was necessary to convince so astute and influential a businessman among our members as Stanley Sagner that there was room and need for an Orthodox synagogue like ours in Pikesville. It was I who had to do the pleading. I convinced him that it would have been an utter waste of energy and money to build another Conservative house of worship only a short distance from the new Chizuk Amuno and Beth El, which between them could easily accommodate those of our people who favored mixed seating and abbreviated services.

I do not expect commendation for having done what I considered to be my duty as the rabbi of Beth Tfiloh who was concerned with its well-being. It is the function of the spiritual leader to prod and stimulate, to plead and set a personal example in giving. To my great satisfaction, my appeals did not fall on deaf ears. Most of those whom I approached for assistance responded magnificently.

At the same time I cannot deny that my preoccupation with the details of the building program compelled me, for at least a decade, to give up all creative scholarly research. Only after the transition from Forest Park to Pikesville was completed and our congregation was well established in its new location, did I resume my investigation into the interpretation of the Bible by the tannaim, that I had begun thirty-five years earlier. It was then that I was in a position also to accept such assignments as the one given me by the editors of the *Encyclopedia Judaica* for the writing of articles that were to appear in that standard reference work of Jewish knowledge, published in Jerusalem in 1971.

Honors Conferred

However, I am running ahead of my account of my personal history. Early in 1960 there began to be conferred upon me one of that series of honors that made me feel that my devotion to the Jewish people and its immortal faith (though it had not been prompted by any desire for reward), was being recognized by the wider community. The Jewish National Fund of Baltimore dedicated its annual banquet for that year to me. It was announced that a forest was being planted in Israel in my name. I had the joy of seeing the beginning of that forest on the outskirts of Jerusalem, when, in the company of Claire and a number of friends, I visited the Jewish homeland for the seventh time. An opportunity to report periodically to the wider Baltimore public on this and other trips was afforded me later on that year as a result of my becoming a weekly columnist for the *Baltimore News-American*.

LXI

Portugal and Spain

OF THESE ANNUAL EXCURSIONS, one of the most exciting was that which took me and Claire to Portugal, Spain, and the island of Majorca in the summer of 1961. I recalled that when I was a child in Hamburg, Germany, the daughter of the second cantor, Dreiblatt, had married a Jewish young man of Lisbon. In order to find out whether she still lived in that city, I inquired about her of the president of the Lisbon Jewish community.

In his reply Professor Amzalak informed me that the lady in question had passed away. However her son, Dr. Semtov Sequerra, would be glad to receive us. When we arrived at the airport this gentleman and his wife were waiting for us. For three days, including the Sabbath, we enjoyed their hospitality. As the Lisbon Kehillah had no rabbi, I was asked to address the young man who was celebrating his Bar Mitzvah that Saturday in Spanish, which was close enough to Portuguese to be understood by him. The event took place in the most exquisite little synagogue I had seen anywhere. Built right after World War Two in a courtyard, the interior of the sanctuary was a combination of marble, gold, and ebony. On Saturday afternoon the maternal uncles of Dr. Sequerra, whom I remembered from my childhood days, came to visit me. We reminisced about the Hamburg that was and sang the old songs that we remembered.

After the outgoing of the Sabbath we were invited to a full-fledged banquet given in honor of the Bar Mitzvah at the Jewish community center. Fully one half of Lisbon Jewry, which totaled about seven hundred souls, turned up for the occasion. There were tears in the eyes of the Sequerras and the Dreiblatts when we left after a three-day sojourn, in the course of which we were given, among other things, a chance to inspect the interior of the most luxurious hotel in the world, which had just been completed, the Lisbon Ritz.

There followed a three-week tour of Spain. It included the major cities of Madrid and Barcelona, with their museums, mausolea, palaces, and other public buildings. In Toledo, the former capital of Castile, we were shown the beautiful little Transito Synagogue, built in the fourteenth century by the banker of King Pedro, Samuel Halevi Abulafia. His name, inscribed on a wall of the shrine in large Hebrew letters, was still legible. In Granada we feasted our eyes on the finest specimen of Moorish architecture extant, the Alhambra Palace. It has recently been proven beyond a doubt that this gem of the art of the Moors was constructed at the instance not of a Moorish sultan of the fourteenth century but of the Jewish vizir of a Moorish ruler of the eleventh century.

Our itinerary encompassed also Cordova, the birthplace of Moses Maimonides; Malaga, the native city of the Hebrew poet and philosopher Solomon ibn Gabirol; and Seville, the seat of Ferdinand and Isabella, during whose reign Columbus sailed across the Atlantic to America. Last but not least we spent a delightful weekend in Gibraltar as the guests of the patriarch of the 250-year-old Jewish community, Mr. Ben Naim. It was altogether a most memorable experience. We were regaled with all sorts of exotic dishes, had a chance to observe the most beautiful type of Jewish family life, and took part in conversations conducted in four languages: English, Spanish, French, and Hebrew.

LXII

Change of Personnel

"A GENERATION GOETH and a generation cometh," said Ecclesiastes. Such is the way of the world. In 1961, Cantor Kotlowitz, who had served our congregation faithfully for twenty-nine years, and with whom I had been working hand in hand, retired. He had by that time passed his sixty-fifth birthday. His place was taken by Cantor Joseph Levine, a very talented young musician, who stayed with us only a year and a half. After an interregnum of another twelve months, Cantor Abraham Denburg of Akron, Ohio, was chosen as the precentor of Beth Tfiloh. With his beautiful rich, bell-like tenor voice and his dignified singing in which he has for the past twelve years been assisted by a well-trained choir under the capable direction of William Milner, he has contributed greatly to the inspiration and beauty of our synagogue services.

Reverend Ruback, who had taken the place of Rev. H. B. Zenitz as sexton of our congregation, though Cantor Kotlowitz's senior by several years, stayed on until his death at the age of eighty-seven in 1972. He had, by virtue of his kindness and learning, been a great asset to our congregation.

Israel, Turkey, and Denmark

In the summer of 1963, Claire and I conducted our fourth tour of Israel. On the way home we visited for the first time the city of Istanbul, Turkey. Its once very flourishing Jewish community had dwindled considerably since the First World War. We had a chance also to spend several days in Denmark. After services on Sabbath in the massive synagogue of Copenhagen, which had been erected in the year 1830, we had the pleasure of being entertained in his home by the chief rabbi. Dr. Melchior was the eighth generation of Jewish spiritual leaders of Copenhagen from the same family. He told us, with relish and delight, how, after the unsuccessful attempt by the Nazis, during their occupation of this little Scandinavian country, to do to the synagogue of Copenhagen what they had done to all others under their jurisdiction, King Christian X, with whom he was very friendly had written him a personal letter of congratulations.

Shortly after our return from abroad, on October 9, to be exact, we were presented with our fourth grandson, Daniel Eli, our David and Jackie's youngest.

Passing of Howard Shpritz

The following year was saddened for us by the premature death, at the age of fifty-two, of our executive director, Howard Shpritz. He had probably more to do with the designing of the complex of buildings on Old Court Road than the builders and planners, Morton Macks, Irving Kroll, and Joseph Lazinsky. However, he was not fortunate enough to see the realization of his dreams.

D. D. Honoris Causa

Ever since my graduation from the Jewish Theological Seminary of America, whereby I became automatically a member of the Rabbinical Assembly, I had, notwithstanding the fact that I disagreed with the majority of my fellow alumni, remained loyal to my alma mater. Remembering my indebtedness for the nurture I had received from my teachers in that outstanding institution of Jewish learning, I had, throughout the years, done my share in raising among the members of my flock funds for its maintenance. In the year 1965 four decades had rolled by since the title of Rabbi, Teacher, and Preacher had been bestowed upon me. So the seminary decided, at its annual graduation in June of that year, to confer upon me the degree of Doctor of Divinity, Honoris Causa. It gave me and my congregation a great deal of satisfaction.

LXIII

Last Year in Forest Park

Marriage of Our Youngest

THE FEELING OF ELATION over this mark of recognition had not yet worn off when Claire and I had further cause for rejoicing. It was when on July 5, exactly a month after the seminary convocation, our youngest son, Josef, became the husband of lovely Marilyn Schoenfeld. He could not possibly, as it was demonstrated repeatedly since, have made a better selection of a life partner.

The marriage of Josef and Marilyn was the last such function in the synagogue of Beth Tfiloh in Forest Park. At the end of January of 1966 our congregation moved, lock, stock, and barrel, to its new location in Pikesville. From that time on—and while the parsonage houses, to be occupied by the rabbi, cantor, and sexton were being built on congregational grounds near the synagogue—we officials had to rough it on Saturdays and holidays. We were compelled to spend the nights on uncomfortable cots in our uncompleted offices and subsist on warmed-over food sent in by caterers. But we bore patiently our exile and our being away from our families on what were supposed to be days of rest, knowing that the situation was bound to end within a foreseeable time.

Death of Mother

In the midst of this hectic period, about a week before Passover, I received word that my mother, whom I had visited only a few days earlier in Lakewood, New Jersey, whither she had moved from New York's East Side the year previous, had passed away. During the thirty-three years since my father's premature death, life had not been

Beth Tfiloh complex 3300 Old Court Road 1966

Interior of Beth Tfiloh's Sanctuary on Old Court Road

too kind to her. She had lost a daughter, my sister Gertrude, when Gertrude was only thirty-six years old. She was next bereaved of her second son, my handsome brother Leo, who died at forty-six. The last blow was the death of Teddy Gruber, the husband of my youngest sister, Sylvia, at the early age of forty-nine. But she accepted tragedy with dignity and stoic fortitude. She had been an avid reader, and was fortunate in retaining her physical faculties and mental alertness until the last day of her life of eighty-six years. Then she went to sleep, never to wake up again. I always felt close to her and deeply mourned her passing.

Moving to Pikesville

The house that was built for us by the congregation was completed on July 14, 1966. Transferring our belongings, especially the library, from our home on Springdale Avenue to our new residence on Old Forest Road, was quite a chore. It took me and a helper seven days to pack my books and three days to set them up again. But once we were installed and everything was in place, we had no difficulty getting acclimated to our new surroundings.

We, of course, took our maid, Lizzie Gaskins, who had been with us since the time of our Josef's Bar-Mitzvah, along with us. Since, however, the nearest bus stop was a mile away from our new home, a task was added to my list of responsibilities, which I believe has not been performed by any rabbi before me, namely, that of picking up the maid almost every day except on the Sabbath and festivals.

The secret of our ability to retain our help as long as we did was that Claire and I always treated them with courtesy and kindness, and interested ourselves in their personal problems. Lizzie's predecessor, Mattie Johnson, a big woman, half Negro and half American Indian, maintained her friendly relations with us, after her retirement because of poor health, until her dying day. Lizzie came to us from the country completely raw and unskilled. She learned a great deal about cooking from Claire. She has been most accommodating and the very soul of honesty and very neat about her person. When her husband died, both Claire and I expected to attend the funeral. However, just on the day when the last rites were to be performed for the departed, our dishwasher went out of order. When, thereupon, Claire informed Lizzie of what had happened and that I would have to remain in the house until the plumber came, there was a moment of silence at the other end of the wire. "Mrs. Rosenblatt," Lizzie asked hesitantly, "would it be all right with you if you waited for the repairman and Dr. Rosenblatt came to the funeral?" Taking the hint Claire replied: "Would you want Dr. Rosenblatt to deliver the eulogy?" "Yes" was Lizzie's timid reply. As it turned out, it was possible for both of us to be present. After the colored preacher, to whom Lizzie's husband had been a total stranger, had spoken for about half an hour, I made a few personal remarks about the deceased, concentrating on the virtues of the man I had known and skipping over his shortcomings. When the service was over, one of the nieces of our maid said to her aunt: "Aunt Lizzie, when my time comes I would want Rabbi Rosenblatt to officiate."

Neither I nor Claire ever harbored racial prejudices. Our views influenced the thinking and demeanor of not only our children but our grandchildren as well. When we were still living in Forest Park, a Negro family moved into the house next-door to ours and our grandsons Jonathan and Aaron frequently played with the children of the neighbors. One day, Aaron, who was not quite four at the time, remarked to Jonathan, who was about two years older: "Jonathan, when Gregory's sister grows up, I am going to marry her." Jonathan's response was: "You can't. She is not Jewish."

The problem of housing for myself and Claire had been most satisfactorily solved. We felt very comfortable in our new home, which had been built according to Claire's own specifications. This did not, however, take care of the needs of our David and his family. In Forest Park they had lived in a house that was just two doors from our own. Every Friday and holiday evening, and often at lunch time on Saturdays, we had eaten together. The very thought that this closeness might be terminated by the distance between us was disturbing. But there was nothing available in the immediate vicinity in Pikesville, and the cost of the homes within walking distance that were for sale, was even then prohibitive. By sheer accident I learned that a couple I knew was about to put their home, which was just two doors away from ours, on sale. I asked them to let David and Jackie see it. Within two weeks the property was bought and our families were reunited. Nothing could have equaled the pleasure that Claire and I have been deriving from this renewed proximity of our dear children and their beloved offspring.

LXIV

Year of the Six-Day War

NINETEEN SIXTY-SEVEN was the year of the Six-Day War. The weeks immediately preceding Israel's third confrontation with its Arab neighbors since its birth in 1948 were filled with nervousness and tension for Jews everywhere. The worst was feared for the land that had awakened the greatest Jewish hopes when hostilities broke out on Monday morning, June 5. Fortunately the outcome was the direct opposite of what had been anticipated. Instead of Israel's being wiped off the map, the territory under its control tripled, extending all the way from the Jordan River in the east to the Suez Canal in the west. Most cheering of all was the fact that Jews were able to pray again without molestation, at what was to them the most sacred spot on earth, the "Wall," the only relic of the Temple of Jerusalem.

Dedication of the New Sanctuary

It was in exaltation of the spirit that we of Beth Tfiloh dedicated our recently completed sanctuary on Sunday, June 25. To the president at the time, Sam Epstein, who had personally watched every nail that was driven in and had negotiated the mortgage at a very reasonable rate of interest, it must have been a particular source of satisfaction. The auditorium was so built as to give the worshippers a feeling of intimacy and closeness. It also had the finest acoustics, so that a microphone was almost unnecessary. My only regret is that I had not been able to prevail upon the builders to effect the same kind of elevation in the section reserved for women as that which existed in the synagogue in Forest Park.

Because of the disturbed situation in Israel during the months preceding, it had been impossible for me to go through with plans of another Israel pilgrimage that summer. So Claire and I spent several weeks again in Mexico.

Expo '67

At the end of August I took my two grandsons, Jonathan and Aaron, who were then respectively eleven and nine, with me to Montreal, Canada, to see Expo 1967. The exhibits were more lavish and beautiful than those of the world exposition in New York several years earlier. But what gave these two youngsters, who were marvelous travel companions, the biggest thrill was to note how their grandfather, by producing his press-card, which had been given to him by the *News-American*, was able to get into the various pavilions without having to wait his turn in the long lines in front of most of them.

A Kosher Dining Room at Hopkins

Shortly before the beginning of the fall semester at the Johns Hopkins University, I received a call from a young law student, who was a recent graduate of the Hopkins School of Arts and Sciences, asking my help in a project that he felt would interest me. Until that time, notwithstanding the fact that the proportion of Jews at the Homewood campus then already constituted twenty-five percent of the total enrollment, and a considerable number of them were committed to the observance of the Jewish dietary laws, there was no kosher dining facility available there, such as had been established by B'nai B'rith at College Park in the vicinity of the University of Maryland. He had collected all the data pertaining to the cost and operating expenses of kosher dining rooms in other American institutions of higher learning, and he felt certain that if I were to approach the authorities of the Johns Hopkins University, they might be persuaded to follow the example set elsewhere. I immediately got in touch with the Hopkins chaplain, Dr. Chester Wickwire, with whom I enjoyed very cordial relations, having participated in the courses on the world's religions organized by him. He proved to be as sympathetic to the undertaking as I had thought he might be. With his encouragement and endorsement, the plans were presented to the officers of the administration in charge of such matters. Within several months a small wing of one of the dormitory buildings that housed the general dormitory cafeteria was converted into a dining room and kitchen, and some sixty students were able to obtain kosher meals right on the university grounds.

LXV

Forty Years of Service

IN THE FALL OF THAT YEAR, four decades had passed since I had been engaged as rabbi of Beth Tfiloh. The banquet in celebration of this milestone in my connection with the congregation was held on January 14 of the year following. It was not necessary to rent a hotel facility, since we had our own spacious and beautiful Stanley Sagner Auditorium. Everything was in readiness for the occasion to which all of Beth Tfiloh looked forward with eager anticipation, when the elements decided to interfere. It had snowed all day Saturday. The ground was covered with ice and sleet. A fierce gale was blowing. Then, on Sunday afternoon, all the lights in the neighborhood went out. The cause of the sudden darkness was the fact that the truck of our caterer had skidded into an electric-power pole, knocking it out completely. One of our friends telephoned us frantically, suggesting that the affair be called off. But it was too late. Furthermore who could tell whether such a situation might not arise again at a later date? So the Gas and Electric Company was contacted and worked feverishly to restore the power.

Because of his preoccupation with them, our executive director, Irving Wiener, had failed to pick up at the airport our guest speaker, Dr. Max Arzt, vice-chancellor of the seminary, who had flown in especially from sunny Florida. Not being too well besides, this representative of my alma mater was fuming as he waited in vain for somebody to get him. On top of that, the driver of the cab he had been advised to take, lost his way in the wilds of snow-covered Pikesville. This was the last straw. When he had finally arrived, he was ready to go right back. It was only Claire's serving him a hot toddy, while trying to calm him, that put him into good humor again.

When the lights had gone out in our banquet hall, the caterer quickly produced candles which were set up on every table. At the appointed hour all but four of the seven hundred persons, who had arranged to attend the dinner, showed up. They thought that the candles had been purposely lit for atmosphere. Then precisely at 7:30 P.M., as the procession of the principals began to move, the electric lights went on again and a marvelous time was had by all. It was another one of those warm, inspiring events that have highlighted my career as Beth Tfiloh's spiritual leader, the memory of which will linger forever in my mind.

Israel's stunning victory of June 1967 made me and Claire all the more anxious to conduct another pilgrimage to the now enlarged Jewish homeland in the summer of 1968, followed by a week's trip through Sweden and Norway via the fiords of the latter. We had the pleasure of visiting, while we were in Jerusalem, Minister Moshe Shapira, the very influential Mizrachi member of the government of Israel. It was upon his insistence that General Moshe Dayan had been taken into the cabinet as minister of defense just prior to the outbreak of the Six-Day War, a step which had contributed in no small measure to Israel's triumph.

In May of 1969, between Passover and the Feast of Weeks, Claire and I conducted another tour to Israel, followed by a short visit to London, England. This time we included in our itinerary the growing new seaport of Elat on the Red Sea, the fortress of Masada overlooking the Dead Sea, the copper mines of Solomon, and the ruins of the Nabatean town of Avdat, as well as Jericho, one of the world's oldest and most frequently rebuilt cities.

The Pride of Grandparents

If the accomplishments of their children are a source of joy to parents, all the more so does this apply to the achievements of grandchildren. When the study of the Torah is pursued diligently by three generations in succession, remarked one of the sages of the Talmud, on the basis of the statement in Isaiah 59:21, it is established in the family forever. Teaching our David any branch of Jewish lore had, from the time that he was a little boy, been pure pleasure. It was even more so when I took his firstborn, Jonathan, in hand and began to instruct him in the Mishnah and other such disciplines. The results of my efforts became evident in his performance on the Sabbath of his Bar Mitzvah, which was celebrated for reasons of convenience on Shabbat B'reshit, the first Saturday after the fall festival season, which fell on October 11. Not only did he uphold the Rosenblatt tradition by the accurate and musically perfect chanting of the texts of the Torah and the Haftarah. He also delighted those present at the luncheon that followed the services by his witty and most appropriate remarks.

On December 27 of that same year Claire and I became grandparents for the fifth time by the birth of Michael, Josef and Marilyn's firstborn. They had just moved into their new home, which was close enough to make it possible for them and their offspring, as soon as they were old enough to walk, to become regular worshippers in our synagogue.

A New Educational Director

In November 1968, Eric Levi, who had for a total of three decades served our schools in every capacity from that of tutor to that of director of all educational activities, resigned his position. During the year that followed, and until the engagement of Rabbi William Shimansky, Mrs. Sarah Lesser, an experienced teacher in the Jewish educational system, filled the vacancy. Rabbi Shimansky was well qualified for his position, and under his able direction our day school in particular made progress again, after the decline in its enrollment which had been caused chiefly by the transition from Forest Park to Pikesville. He was well entrenched by the year 1970.

Bar Mitzvah of Daniel Isaac

It was in May of that year that our second grandson, Daniel Isaac, the son of Judah and Lisa, celebrated his Bar Mitzvah. He and his parents came from Cleveland, and his maternal grandparents from New York, for the occasion. It was a treat to hear him perform, just as his cousin had eight months previously, in our synagogue in his musical alto voice.

Associate Rabbi Chosen

Before Claire and I went to Israel, Rome, and Madrid for our summer vacation that year, our congregation had engaged as my associate Rabbi Nissim Wernick of Atlanta, Georgia. To a certain extent I was personally responsible for this development. I had on a number of occasions indicated that, as the time was approaching when I would have to be relieved of at least some of my responsibilities, it would be wise to groom a younger man, who would eventually take my place so that a congregation of the size of ours would not be left like sheep without a shepherd. After having been with us for half a year, Rabbi Wernick severed his connection with us in order to assume a post with a congregation in Dallas, Texas.

President of the Baltimore Zionist Federation

He was still serving us when the Zionist parties of Baltimore, in keeping with a movement that was nationwide, formed an umbrella organization to be known as the Baltimore Zionist Federation. I was prevailed upon to serve as its first president. I accepted the assignment only upon being assured of the cooperation of my fellow officers. If, during my administration it was possible in 1971 to run a well-patronized concert in honor of Israel Independence Day, and a year later a most successful Israel fair, both in our synagogue premises, it was because this promise was kept and I was able to secure the collaboration of the entire Zionist family of Baltimore.

At the end of November 1970 Beth Tfiloh observed the golden jubilee of its founding by a series of outstanding and inspiring functions. It had by that time recouped some of the losses in membership due to the transfer from Forest Park.

Our day school, as noted before, was continuing to attract pupils. However, because of the necessity of increasing the tuition fees in keeping with rising costs, some parents, too proud to ask for reductions, withheld from enrolling their children. In order to meet this situation, I had long urged the raising of a scholarship fund, to which parents of pupils who were not affiliated with Beth Tfiloh, and outsiders in general, who recognized the importance of Jewish education, would contribute. I found an ardent supporter in Dr. Charles Siegel, an outstanding physician of our city and a dedicated Jew, who had assumed the responsibility of president of the PTA. Unfortunately he passed away all too soon. But his wholesome influence is still felt. The foundation he laid is being built upon, and scores of our youth, who might otherwise have been deprived of an intensive Jewish education, are the beneficiaries.

In 1971

At the beginning of 1971 there took place again, in the vital office of executive director of our congregation, another change of the guard. Simultaneously with Rabbi Wernick, Irving Wiener, who had played a major role in his engagement, gave up his position. His place was taken by Harold Hammer, a kind, affable person who had served in the capacity of coordinator of activities in other congregations. He was on the staff of Beth Tfiloh when our youngest grandson, the second son of Josef and Marilyn, was born. Also, when our third grandson, Aaron, celebrated his Bar Mitzvah on Saturday, August 7, he saw to it that everything ran smoothly. Like his older brother, Jonathan, Aaron acquitted himself extremely well in chanting the weekly portion as well as the message from the Prophets.

Vacation in Switzerland, Italy, and Austria

That summer Claire and I did not travel to Israel. Instead we drove with a few intimate friends through beautiful Switzerland, the north of Italy, and the mountains of Tyrol as far east as Vienna. On the way from picturesque Salzburg, where we listened to a modern opera in the world-renowned Mozart Theater, we visited the former Mauthausen concentration camp, where thousands of Jews had been tortured to death during the Hitler era. It was a most *traumatic* experience.

LXVI

At Three Score and Ten

I WAS NOW APPROACHING what, according to Scripture, is the average human life-span. "The days of our years," says the psalmist," are three-score years and ten." The time had come, so I thought, when I ought to be able to take things a little easier. I had no intention, so long as the Almighty would give me health and the ability to function, of withdrawing completely from what had been the scene of my activities for four and a half decades. First of all I felt it was not good for a man, who had been active all his life, suddenly to allow everything he had been doing to come to a stop. It would have a devastating effect upon him, incapacitating him from giving what he still had to offer. Secondly, it would deprive those he serves of the benefits of his experience, for which there is no substitute. It was my desire to continue, so long as I had the strength, as senior rabbi of Beth Tfiloh.

But when I was informed that no candidate of stature would be willing to accept the pulpit of a congregation like ours unless he was assured of being number one, I agreed to the title of rabbi emeritus, provided that I occupy the pulpit periodically, perform whatever private services might be asked of me, and be free to express my views. In short it was made crystal clear that, however my status might be construed, I would be a rabbi emeritus who was not only visible, but also "audible and active." With this understanding, preparations were made for the banquet in celebration of my seventieth birthday and the presentation at that same time, to our congregation and the Jewish community of Baltimore in general, of my successor, Dr. David Novak of Oklahoma City. The date chosen for the "occasion extraordinaire" was Sunday, June 1. In the services of the Sabbath preceding this gala function, my

Seated from left to right: Samuel and Claire. Standing from left to right: grandson Aaron, daughter-in-law Marilyn, daughter-in-law Lisa, son Judah, son David, grandson Daniel, son Josef, daughter-in-law Jaclyn, grandson Jonathan

grandchildren as well as my children played their role. However, the highlight in the proceedings of that morning was the sermon delivered by my grandson Jonathan, who had already then made up his mind to prepare for the rabbinate. The love and reverence for his grandfather that this not yet sixteen-year-old youth, who was an honor student at the Talmudical Academy of Baltimore, expressed in his address, were such that there was not a dry eye among the hundreds of worshippers in the synagogue on that day.

On the Sunday evening following there prevailed, at the dinner held in the Stanley Sagner Auditorium, which was filled to capacity, a mood of festivity and warmth of friendship that is rare indeed. No public servant could have asked for a greater outpouring of the hearts nor for a more genuine recognition of the work of a lifetime than the accolades I received that evening, and the sincere joy, mingled with sorrow, displayed by all who were present.

LXVII

Epilogue

I HAVE TRIED, in the preceding pages, to give a summary of the principal events revolving about me in the course of the first seven decades of my life. It is time now to pause for an evaluation, a consideration of what fifty years in the active rabbinate have taught me about the profession I had chosen when I was a young child, and to the practice of which I had been dedicated so long.

That the chief function of the rabbi is to teach goes without saying. The original and literal meaning of the word is "teacher," and only he is qualified to impart knowledge to others who is thoroughly acquainted with his subject of instruction. In the case of the spiritual leader of a Jewish congregation in present-day America, however, what is required of him, in order to be effective in his calling, is not only familiarity with his Jewish sources. He must also be well versed in the culture of the world around him and keep abreast of the times in which he lives, so as to be in a position to interpret the traditions of Judaism to make them relevant to the current needs of his flock.

Yet erudition, Jewish as well as secular, however wide it be, coupled with the finest gifts for making ideas articulate, is not enough to render the listeners to the occupant of the pulpit responsive to his appeals and his efforts to influence and persuade them. In order to inspire them to follow his leadership and react positively to his direction, he, to whom they look for guidance must possess certain ethical qualities without which all his preaching would remain but a "voice calling in the wilderness."

First among the attributes that I believe a spiritual leader ought to possess is integrity, his deeds matching his words. People find out very quickly whether the individual whom they have selected as their mentor is sincere or not. Once they discover that he is not what he pretends to be, they are turned off, and regardless of what he may say and how well he may say it, they pay no further attention to him.

Secondly, in order to lead, he who aspires for such a role must be a man of principle, one who will stand up and fight for his ideals regardless of the opposition he may encounter. He must be a person who will not sell his birthright for a mess of pottage. He may make enemies among those he crosses, but he will, at least, be respected by them.

Thirdly, just as a father must, in order not to cause jealousy among his children, give the same measure of love to each and every one of them, so must the spiritual father of his flock treat all his congregants alike, not discriminating between rich or poor, powerful or insignificant. He must show a deep interest in the personal problems of all who turn to him for help. I always considered it to be my function to serve as a unifying force rather than as a cause of division in the congregation. That is why I never allowed myself to be drawn into synagogue politics by taking sides in the annual elections. Whenever I noted the possibility of a rift—and that happened on a number of occasions—I acted as a conciliator, averting a split that would have been detrimental to the congregation's well-being and its ability to render the services for which it had been established.

Fourthly, he must possess the trait of humility. It is not necessary for him who stands at the head of his community to be arrogant in order to command respect. On the contrary, it is by the human warmth he exhibits toward those he aspires to lead that a leader gains a following while arrogance, the exaltation of his own ego, repels and begets hatred.

These were the standards I had set for myself, the ideals I endeavored to realize, the guidelines I tried to follow. Whether I succeeded is for others to judge. I always took my function as preacher seriously enough to prepare as thoroughly as I could whenever I rose to speak in public. Never did I underestimate the intelligence of my audience. My philosophy was that of the celebrated actor who said, "Whenever I perform, I make believe that I am playing before the king."

Though I started out as a student, who is usually a recluse far removed from ordinary mundane affairs, I learned—and it did not come easy—that the most eloquent and erudite lecture cannot take the place of a single act of human kindness, of personal concern and attention, especially in times of trouble.

While, of course, I responded to the call of every member of my flock in weal as well as woe without distinction, I would make it my business to go out of my way when those who were not particularly favored by Providence needed my services.

Furthermore, I always put principle above expediency, but if I had to take a definite stand on behalf of "the Lord and His Torah," I never singled out any individual for reprimand or criticism. Knowing that no human being is perfect, that every mortal has his shortcomings, I tried to see in each and every member of my flock what was good in him and develop his positive qualities, overlooking his inadequacies and deficiencies.

Last, but not least, though I had been chosen to lead, I never considered my opinion the last word on every subject. I realized that in worldly matters laymen might be greater experts than I.

If my ministry, which has by now extended over half a century, has met with some measure of success, it is due to large measure to this conception that I entertained of my duties—this in addition to a sort of intuitively cheerful outlook on life. Claire often called me an incurable optimist. This optimism may, to a great extent, have been the result of the many favors showered upon me by the Creator from the time of my birth. I was most fortunate in having been born of parents like my saintly father and my angelic mother. I have, on the whole, enjoyed very good health, rarely being compelled by illness to miss the performance of my responsibilities or duties. I was blessed in having secured a mate like Claire, who not only sweetened my life, but by her advice and counsel brought out the best in me. The children she bore me, and the partners they selected and the offspring they begat, have been sources of pure and unadulterated satisfaction to me and her. It was my good fortune, also, that after one year in Trenton, New Jersey, I became the rabbi of the Beth Tfiloh Congregation, which I have served ever since. It was not less providential that shortly after my arrival in Baltimore I was able to make connections with the Johns Hopkins University, the Semitics department of which was a few years later headed for three whole decades by that prince among scholars, W. F. Albright.

I have been honored by almost every organization in which I have been active, though I never sought emolument. I was the recipient of the B'nai B'rith Menorah Lodge's Simchah Award, of the Sidney Hollander Award of the Baltimore branch of the American Jewish Congress, of the Chief Rabbi Isaac Halevi Herzog Fellowship Gold

Medal of the National American Mizrachi, over the local branch of which I have presided for a total of ten years. I have also received Baltimore Hadassah's Myrtle Wreath. I was tendered testimonials for my services to the Jewish students at the Johns Hopkins University and to the Vaad Hakashruth of Baltimore, by the Talmudical Academy of Baltimore, and by the Maccabean Post of Jewish Veterans of our city. I have been sent on missions on behalf of the Ner Israel Rabbinical College as well as the world Religious Zionist movement. I have, as much as it is humanly possible, seen the fulfillment of almost all my heart's desires. Therefore I have every reason, now that I have passed the proverbial three-score and ten of the "days of my years," to feel grateful to the Almighty for having permitted me to live and serve.